Yvonne L.
1612 W. Susa
Missoula, Montana
59801
Nov. 1976

The pendant design with the circle, ellipse and rectangle as the central motif

JEWELRY
MAKING *and* DESIGN

An illustrated textbook
for Teachers, Students of Design and
Craft Workers

BY

AUGUSTUS F. ROSE *and*

ANTONIO CIRINO, B.S.

FOURTH REVISED EDITION

DOVER PUBLICATIONS, INC.
NEW YORK

Published in Canada by General Publishing Company, Ltd., 30 Lesmill Road, Don Mills, Toronto, Ontario.
Published in the United Kingdom by Constable and Company, Ltd., 10 Orange Street, London WC 2.

This Dover edition, first published in 1967, is a revised and enlarged version of the work published by The Davis Press, Inc., in 1949.

International Standard Book Number: 0-486-21750-7

Library of Congress Catalog Card Number: 66-29501

Manufactured in the United States of America
Dover Publications, Inc.
180 Varick Street
New York, N. Y. 10014

DEDICATION

While the first revised edition of "Jewelry Making and Design" was in press, the co-author, Augustus Foster Rose, was laid to rest, after a life of intelligent devotion to a phase of education he so eminently sponsored.

His skilled hands, alert mind, and inspiring enthusiasm did much toward advancing the metalwork and jewelry making crafts to their present high place in our educational program. In tribute to Mr. Rose as a great teacher and director of manual arts, and leader in the field of metalcraft and jewelry design, the co-author respectfully dedicates this revised edition.

Antonio Cirino

Foreword

TO THE DOVER EDITION

IT IS very gratifying to the author that a continuing demand for *Jewelry and Jewelry Making* has given rise to a new edition of this book. For a number of years the book has been very hard to find, and many persons who wished to obtain it have been disappointed to learn that it was not available.

The first edition of this book was published in 1918. A second revised edition was published in 1946, and a third revised edition in 1949. This Dover edition is thus the fourth edition. It differs from the 1949 edition in that it contains two chapters on cuff links and cuff buttons which appeared in the second edition but were unwisely omitted from the third. Likewise it contains about thirty-six illustrations that appeared in the 1946 but not the 1949 edition. Entirely new to this edition is the list of Additional Reference Books which begins on page 302.

Earlier editions of this book featured several full-color illustrations; these appear in this Dover edition in black and white, since it was not possible to reproduce them in color at reasonable cost.

Previous editions of this work were all extremely limited in size and rather expensive. It is my hope that this new, economical and more generally available edition will be useful to students, amateur craftsmen and professional jewelers throughout the world, many of whom have been kind enough to express their admiration for the work as a basic textbook in this branch of the metal arts.

ANTONIO CIRINO

East Providence, Rhode Island
July, 1966

Foreword

TO THE THIRD EDITION

THE subject of jewelry is treated in this book from an educational standpoint, and is presented as a series of progressive lessons consecutively arranged from the simple to the complex. The authors have practiced the methods laid down in the book and have obtained satisfactory results. They have tried to present the subject in a way that will be helpful to those who are beginning the work and to suggest ideas for those who have passed beyond the amateur stage.

An abundance of illustrated material will be found, consisting of drawings, designs and photographs of finished work, executed by students of all ages, including the High School, the Art School and the Professional Craftsman.

The various materials and processes involved are described in detail, and the necessary equipment for individual or for school use is outlined and illustrated.

The numerous designs in the book are shown with the idea of leading the student to think and design for himself and not to copy. Deliberate copying checks the student's development and stunts his individuality.

ACKNOWLEDGMENTS

The authors wish to thank the following persons and companies who have assisted in the successful completion of this book: Mr. F. E. Masselin, for assistance with the chapter on "Modeling and Casting"; Metal Crafts Supply Company, Providence, Rhode Island, for the illustrations of tools and equipment; Dumore Company, Racine, Wisconsin, for the illustration of a high-speed precision drill on page 146; G. & C. Merriam Company, Springfield, Mass., for technical definitions of styles of stone cutting on pages 4 and 5; Rhode Island School of Design for the use of their facilities in developing the work treated in this book; and former students whose drawings and designs are reproduced.

TABLE OF CONTENTS

Book I. Jewelry Making

Book II. Jewelry Design

Introduction

THE Making of Jewelry is an ancient art, and may be traced to a very remote period, not only by examples, of which there are many, but through ancient writings. Abundant examples of goldsmiths' work have been found in Egyptian tombs dating as far back as the fifteenth century B.C. The Bible has many references to the use of jewelry.

The goldsmiths' craft, as practiced centuries ago, has many attractive features that may be adapted or applied to the craft work of the present time. The possibilities for the application of design are unlimited. With no other material can more satisfactory results be obtained in the finished piece of work than with that employed by the goldsmith. No other craft calls for such skill in the handling of the materials used, or so keen a sense of fine line and proportion in design.

Jewelry comprises various objects for personal adornment, rendered precious by their workmanship. In the form of rings and pendants, jewelry may be merely decorative, or in the form of brooches and pins, it may be useful as well. The making of jewelry cultivates an appreciation of this ancient art. To acquire the keenest sense of appreciation for the fine jewelry of ancient or modern times, one must study the designs as expressed in the work, and practice the art. The knowledge derived from actual practice is both cultural and practical. It not only helps to develop the artistic impulse and make the individual sensitive to the beauty of nature as applied to metal, but it also arouses interest in the metal industries and the commercial processes allied with the manufacture of jewelry on a large scale, such as mining, assaying and alloying.

The pieces of jewelry most prized by our museums today are those made centuries ago, where cleverness in design and workmanship were of much greater value than the material used.

Many craftsmen design in the material, feeling their way along without a drawing, but, as Benvenuto Cellini says, "Though many have practised the art without making drawings, those who made their drawings first did the best work."

In school work we have our attention called very often to the work of architects, sculptors, painters and engineers, but mention is seldom made of those who have worked in metal, even though their work represents some of the finest moments in the history of mankind. Few know that Tubal Cain was the first metal worker of whom we have any record, or that Bezaleel of the Tribe of Judah and Oholiab of the Tribe of Dan were the goldsmiths who made the sacred jewels and vessels for the tabernacle. The names of Mentor, Acrages, Stratonicus, Unichus, and Hecataeus are unknown to many, but these are the men who produced the superb Greek specimens in metal, many of which are now to be seen in our museums. During the middle ages, it was the custom for each of the kings of France to have his goldsmith. Gilbert Lorin was goldsmith to Charles the Seventh, Jehan Gallant to Charles the Eighth, and Henri to Louis the Twelfth. Few know that our honored patriot, Paul Revere, was a worker in the precious metals.

At the beginning, jewelry making occupied a jealous and important position in the field of the goldsmiths' craft. As early as the Twelfth Century, the goldsmiths of Florence made articles of great variety to answer multifarious needs of a sensitive people. Articles in silver and gold for church services, and for household and personal use, challenged the skills and ingenuity of the creative artist.

The demands for everyday needs called for a great variety of materials, such as gold, silver, bronze, marble, wood and clay. The Florentine craftsman knew all the intricate processes of casting, hammering, chiseling, filing, sawing, and carving. Not infrequently the commission involved a synthesizing of metals and textiles, as in a brocade, or of stone and painting, as in mosaic—and jewelry setting. There being intense commercial rivalry in those days, ipso facto, the craftsman was compelled to resort to astute design and ingenuity for originality and economy of production. For aesthetic quality to be of the highest, he employed the principles of design with complete understanding and superlative mastery. Skillful use of form, color, composition, perspective, harmony, taste, and beauty, gave to technical performance, grandeur and sumptuousness.

Scientific knowledge, technical skill, and aesthetic conception made up a large part of the craftsman's equipment. With this he stood in readiness to challenge all difficulties. It is, indeed, little wonder to the research scholar that the training and education of the Florentine goldsmith constituted such a complete cosmos of experiences, knowledge, and skills. To this craftsman no order was too small or any difficulty too great.

To the scholar searching for what made Florentine art great, history reveals that its painters, sculptors and architects were, or had been, goldsmiths. History tells that Orcagna, 1349, listed as a painter was a Florentine goldsmith; that Ghiberti, the builder of the Paradise Doors, so called, was a goldsmith; that Brunelleschi, although he spent much time building palaces and churches, was a veritable goldsmith. Each was a goldsmith but, as it happens, the first is classified as a painter, the second as a sculptor, and the third as an architect. To these may be added Donatello, famous as sculptor, but trained as a goldsmith. Then, Verrocchio, equally famous with Donatello as sculptor was also an accomplished goldsmith. The name of Ghirlandajo should be linked with Donatello, as goldsmith, for in the shops of these two, history records that the great Leonardo da Vinci and Michaelangelo served their apprenticeships as craftsmen. The list of such illustrious craftsmen would not be complete without the name of the inimitable masterworker of metals, Benvenuto Cellini.

To him Michaelangelo wrote, "My dear Benvenuto: I have known you for many years as the greatest goldsmith of whom we have any information; and henceforth I shall know you for a sculptor of like quality."

The Florentine craftsman, be he goldsmith, jeweler, weaver, potter, iron or woodworker, was a highly disciplined person. Mastery, thoroughness, skillfulness, and general efficiency marked these craftsmen as important members of the community.

We have limited our discussion to Italian masters, but it would be wrong to conclude that the goldsmith-painter-sculptor-architect relationship was not to be found elsewhere. Two outstanding examples of this relationship are Albrecht Dürer, in Germany, and William Hogarth, in England, both of whom served as apprentices in goldsmith shops.

It would not be overrating the virtues inherent in the nature of jewelry making as a craft to say that as a means and form of education it is very rich in opportunities for fostering good work habits and sound mental disciplines.

Book I
JEWELRY MAKING

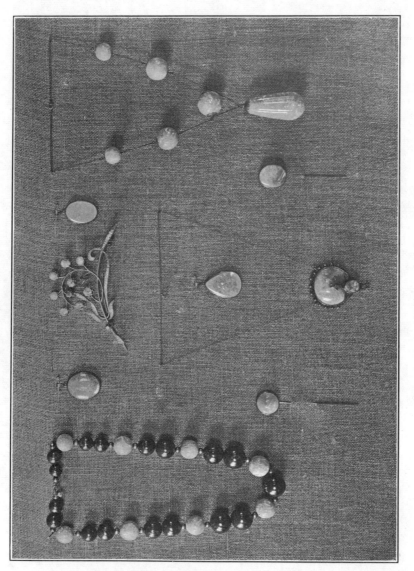

The opals shown here weigh 514 karats and are valued at over $2,500. They are about one-fourth full size

CHAPTER 1

Materials and Methods Used in Jewelry Making

STONES have been worn upon the person since prehistoric times and in most jewelry, stones play the principal part; usually the central feature around which is the ornamentation.

Stones used in jewelry are precious and semiprecious. The value of a stone is merely what it will bring in the open market and its artistic merits may be only a matter of aesthetic judgment.

Stones are only minerals taken from the earth, improved with artistry by cutting and polishing; the finest and rarest of them are called gems.

PRECIOUS STONES

The most precious stones are the diamonds, emeralds, rubies and sapphires. The pearl is oftentimes classed with precious stones. Strictly speaking, it is not a stone but it does hold an honored place in jewelry.

DIAMONDS were originally found in India but are now found in South Africa, Brazil and many other places. The diamond possesses more desirable qualities than other stones and is found in a variety of colors, such as white, black, yellow, brown, blue, green and in many other shades. It is found in deposits of gravel, sand or clay, and in river beds.

EMERALDS are probably the rarest of all precious stones and are considered even more valuable than the diamond. The emerald is found in the rock in which it was formed and unlike diamonds, it never occurs in gem gravels. The best

stones are found in Columbia, South America, but some have
been found in the United States.

The usual shade of color seen in emeralds is alluded to as
emerald green, but the shades most highly valued are those
of an intense fresh green.

RUBIES are the oldest or first known of all precious
stones dating back in early history. The best specimens,
found in Upper Burma, are a shade of red slightly inclined to
the purple and are often called "Pigeon Blood Ruby." Those
found in Ceylon, Siam and Australia do not have this deep,
rich color.

The genuine ruby is obtained from the mineral known
as corundum and contains irregularly shaped bubbles. The
imitation ruby contains bubbles that are perfectly round.
Emery is an impure form of corundum. All genuine stones
contain certain flaws and the fewer the flaws the rarer the
gem. The imperfections in an imitation stone are less noticeable as the manufacturer is more careful than nature.

SAPPHIRES are found in many parts of the world, usually
in the same locality as the ruby. The largest number and
finest quality come from Siam. It is next to the diamond in
hardness and, like the ruby, its value is determined by its
color and quality. The finest stones are a deep blue but
some have been found in other colors such as red, green,
yellow and pink.

PEARLS have been considered from the earliest times
among the most splendid gems. The finest quality pearls are
produced by the pearl mollusk. The people of India and
Persia were among the earliest to collect them because of the
fisheries of Ceylon and the Persian Gulf. Pearl fishing has
been carried on in Ceylon since 550 B.C., and is conducted
much the same today as it was then.

Pearls assume every color of the rainbow. Those with a
rich warm tint are most in demand. The lustre is its chief
characteristic and when combined with the right colors, it is
beautiful and valuable.

SEMIPRECIOUS STONES

A large number of stones used in jewelry are semiprecious; the most important ones being:

NAME	COLOR
Alexandrite	grass green—combined red color
Amethyst	pale purple
Aquamarine	sea green
Chrysoberyl	yellow—pale green
Lapis Lazuli	deep blue
Moonstone	pearly—opaline lustre
Opal	opalescent—fire redness
Peridot	deep yellow-green
Topaz	transparent—pale yellow
Tourmaline	transparent—pink or green
Turquoise	blue
Zircon	blue-green

Others of less importance are:

Agate	reddish—yellow red
Azurite	blue
Bloodstone	green with red
Chrysoprase	translucent green
Coral	red
Carnelian	deep red, flesh red or reddish white
Garnet	red
Jade	green—white, yellow, black, pink and gray
Malachite	green

These stones while comparatively common and inexpensive, are indispensable to the worker in jewelry. The variety of colors in these stones makes it possible to produce unusual designs of artistic merit and to adapt them to the personality and costume of the wearer.

To become acquainted with stones it is best to see and handle them by making a private collection. By adding two or three from time to time and looking each one up in the numerous books on Mineralogy or Gems they become fixed in the mind so that they can be called by name and described at will. This information can prompt research into new areas of knowledge.

STONE CUTTING

Genius discovered that by cutting stones and by polishing, beauty could be added to their form, and lustre to their color. The earliest form of cutting was probably nothing more than an attempt to adapt its outline to the form of setting designed for it by rounding off its corners and other irregularities.

Ludwig Van Berguen of Bruges was the first man to cut the diamond with a symmetrical arrangement of facets.

STYLES IN STONE CUTTING

There are five styles of stone cutting that have been practiced for a long time which are as follows: Cabochon, Table, Rose, Brilliant, and Step or Trap.

STONE CUTTING DEFINITIONS

*CABOCHON—a stone cut in convex form, highly polished but not faceted.

*TABLE—the upper flat surface of a diamond or other precious stone, the sides of which are cut in angles, especially the large flat facet on the top of a brilliant. The upper flat facet of a precious stone.

*ROSE—a form in which diamonds and other gems are cut, used especially when the loss to the stone in cutting it, as a brilliant, would be too great. Typically, the rose cut has a flat circular base and facets in two ranges rising to a point.

*By permission. From *Webster's New International Dictionary*, Second Edition, copyright 1934, 1939, 1945, by G. & C. Merriam Company.

*BRILLIANT—a diamond or other gem cut in a particular form with numerous facets so as to have especial brilliancy. The ordinary modern form resembles two cones placed base to base, the upper part truncated comparatively near its base and the lower having the apex only cut off. It has at the top a principal face, called the table, surrounded by a number of sloping facets forming the bezel or crown, at the bottom it has a small flat facet called culet, parallel to the table and connected with the girdle by a pavilion of elongated facets. Ordinary brilliant has, besides the table and culet, 56 facets, 32 above the girdle and 24 below.

*TRAP—a brilliant so cut that the bezel and the pavilion are each divided into two parts with slightly indifferent slopes.

*STEP—a cut for diamonds or more especially colored stones forming a series of straight facets which decrease in length as they recede from the girdle and so give appearance of steps.

The oldest of these styles of cutting is the rounded \or cabochon which was first used in cutting of rubies, emeralds, sapphires and garnets. Almost all transparent stones are cut with facets.

Opaque and semiopaque stones are cut cabochon, and although the finest cuttings require experience, the amateur will be surprised to find that with a very limited equipment he is able to do creditable cutting.

STONE SLITTING

A piece of rough stone is first closely examined to determine the best method of cutting for the greatest value and the least waste. If the stone is large, it is then slit as illustrated by fig. 1. Next, it is held against the edge of a thin metal disc or circular plate which is primed with fine emery and oil to hasten the separation.

---

*By permission. From *Webster's New International Dictionary*, Second Edition, copyright 1934, 1939, 1945, by G. & C. Merriam Company.

Roughing

After the large lump has been slit up into pieces of the required size and thickness, one of the pieces is held with the fingers against a corundum wheel and roughed into shape. The face to be the front of the stone is then fastened to the end of a holder with cement, which is easily heated over a gas or alcohol flame.

Polishing

If a wheel similar to the ones shown in the following illustrations is used, a few discs of No. 000 sandpaper may be fastened to the side for the finer cutting and polishing. The stone is now held next to the revolving sandpaper disc (fig. 2, page 8) and cut to the required shape. It will be found that the cutting wears away the sandpaper leaving it quite smooth, which is just the surface needed for the polishing. Continuing to hold the stone against the smooth paper with the aid of the powder that has already adhered to the wheel, the stone is given the required polish. Unless it is desired to have a perfectly flat back the stone is given a slight rocking motion during the polishing process. To give the final finish to the stone it is held against a buff with a little putty powder or oxide of tin (bottom illustration, page 8).

After the back is completed, the stone is removed from the stick with the blade of a knife. In doing so, care must be exercised not to chip the stone. The cement is now warmed again and the stone fastened to it, having the face or front of the stone at the top. The cutting is done as before except that the front of the stone is usually rounded more or less which gives it the cut style cabochon (upper illustration, page 9). An ordinary grindstone may be used for the rough cutting and where several stones are to be cut the same size, grooves are made in the grindstone for this purpose.

Some of the semiprecious gem minerals may be obtained at little cost and where the craftsman can do his own

FIGURE 1. Slitting the stone

cutting he is able to save money on his stones, and often-times get results that arc distinctive.

GOLD

Gold is one of the metals taken from the earth and is probably the first known to man. Its first use has been traced back to 3600 B.C.

It is widely distributed in nature and is found in many ways and in all parts of the world; also it was used at a very early period for the construction of personal ornaments. The universal use of gold in preference to all other metals is due to its many properties; its color, lustre, malleability and indestructibility. Gold does not tarnish nor can it be destroyed.

Pure gold, being too soft for all ordinary purposes, is generally alloyed with other metals. Silver and copper are the principal alloys used.

Figure 2. Shaping contour of back

Figure 3. Polishing contour of back

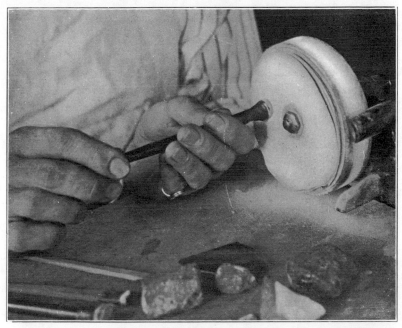

FIGURE 4. Giving final finish to the stone

FIGURE 5. Showing stones in rough and polished state

KARAT

Gold is known by karat. The word "karat" is derived from the seed of the Abyssinian coral tree which is said to be the original karat weight of jewelers. Jewelers and assayers divide the troy pound, ounce or other weight into twenty-four parts and call each a karat as a means of stating the proportion of pure gold contained in any alloy of gold with other metals. Thus, pure gold is considered as 24 karat fine; if two, six, or ten twenty-fourths of alloy is present the gold is said to be 22, 18 or 14 karat fine.

Gold above 18 karat is used only for special work. Eighteen karat and 14 karat are best for most jewelry as they are harder and their wearing qualities better. Various colors of gold may be produced by alloying the gold with varying proportions of silver, copper, or iron.

SILVER

Silver is widely diffused but is rarely found in the native state. It is originally as widespread as gold, occurring in nearly all of the volcanic rocks. Whereas, gold remains unaltered by the action of the elements and is often carried long distances from its place of origin, silver, on the contrary, is only to be found in the rocks where it originated.

Pure silver has a brilliant white color and is the whitest of all metals. None surpasses it in lustre, and in hardness it ranges between pure gold and pure copper. It is more fusible than copper or gold, melting at a bright heat or at 1761°F. It is commonly used for the purpose of alloying gold in its pure state, but if too much be added it makes the gold pale.

It is almost as plastic as pure gold and is too soft to make durable objects that require lightness and stability of form. This defect is overcome by alloying it with a little copper.

An alloy of 925 parts fine silver and 75 parts copper is called 925–1000 fine or what is commonly known as sterling

silver.   This alloy is used almost universally for jewelry and
the best silverware.

The word "sterling" is the quality mark for the best
in silver.   The word is Middle English, probably Anglo-
Saxon.   The origin of the term dates back to the 12th century when five free towns banded together in the eastern
part of Germany calling themselves the Hanseatic League.
They were free to make their own laws and issue their own
currency.   When trading with British merchants, they paid
for the British products with silver coins.   These coins
attracted the attention of the Britishers for their consistency
of metal and dependability of weights and were, therefore,
referred to as the coins of the Esterlings.   In due time, after
the British adopted the characteristics of these coins, the
metal and the coin became known as sterling.   Down to the
present day this term has stood for the test of fineness and
quality.

Melting Points and Specific Gravity of the Principal Metals

Metal	Melting Point Fahrenheit	Melting Point Centigrade	Specific Gravity
Platinum*	3224	1773	21.45
Nickel	2645	1452	8.85
Gold	1945	1063	19.36
Copper	1981	1083	8.94
Silver	1761	960	10.56
Sterling	1688	920	10.40
Coin	1634	890	10.35
Zinc	787	419	7.14
Lead	621	327	11.36
Tin	450	232	7.29

*Infusible, except by the oxy-hydrogen blow pipe.

GENERALLY ACCEPTED LIST OF BIRTHSTONES

January—Garnet
February—Amethyst
March—Aquamarine or Bloodstone
April—Diamond
May—Emerald
June—Pearl or Moonstone
July—Ruby
August—Peridot or Sardonyx
September—Sapphire
October—Opal or Tourmaline
November—Topaz
December—Turquoise or Lapis Lazuli

FINENESS OF GOLD KARATS

1K.	.0417	9K.	.3750	17K.	.7083
2K.	.0833	10K.	.4167	18K.	.7500
3K.	.1250	11K.	.4583	19K.	.7917
4K.	.1667	12K.	.5000	20K.	.8333
5K.	.2083	13K.	.5417	21K.	.8750
6K.	.2500	14K.	.5833	22K.	.9167
7K.	.2917	15K.	.6250	23K.	.9583
8K.	.3333	16K.	.6667	24K.	1.0000

CHAPTER 2

Processes Involved in Jewelry Making

THERE are different ways of approaching the subject of jewelry making. Some begin by having the student or beginner take for the first problem one that calls for the use of wire bending and soldering. Others give a problem calling for the introduction of a variety of processes in one piece. Experience shows that the best and most satisfactory results are obtained both from the student's point of view and the consideration of the finished product when the student is led to advance from the simple problem to the more complex by a series of elementary problems carefully graded. The beginner has not only to learn the processes involved in the making of a piece of jewelry but also to master the various tools used and to learn the limitations of his material. Although the number of tools used in jewelry making are few, it seems best for the beginner to take them up one or two at a time and plan his problem accordingly.

The processes involved in jewelry making are as follows:

Sawing	Polishing
Filing	Coloring
Bending	Pickling
Carving	Modeling
Embossing or repoussé	Casting
Soldering	Annealing
Stone Setting	

Each of these will be taken up and explained in the various problems that follow.

Perforated silver brooches with simple patterns

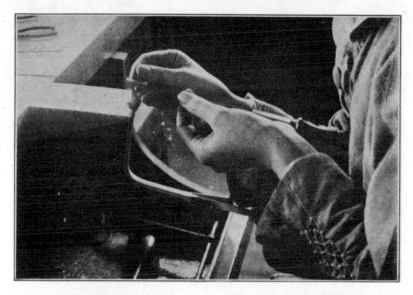

FIGURE 6. Position of saw frame while inserting the saw blade

the problem is carried out. After the tracing is made we take a piece of twenty gauge silver a little larger than the design calls for. A drop of liquid glue is placed on the metal and, after diluting it by adding two or three drops of water, it is spread over the surface of the metal and made quite thin. The thinner the glue the greater the adhesion. The tracing is then placed on the silver and allowed to dry. Paste is not satisfactory. The tracing should not be pulled either one way or the other as it tends to stretch and distort the design.

After the tracing is dry, a center punch is used to make small depressions in each of the openings to be pierced as a start for the drill. A drill of the right size for the opening is then selected and placed in the chuck and the holes made to admit the saw. The saw frame is held as shown in fig. 6 and a No. 0 saw is fastened in the end of the frame nearest the handle so that the teeth of the saw are on the upper edge and point toward the handle of the frame. The saw is then allowed to pass through one of the holes in the piece

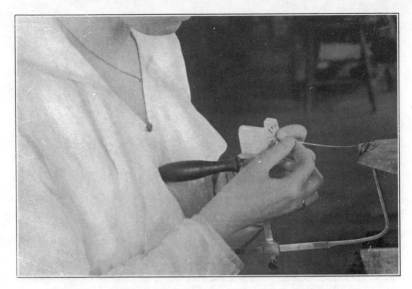

FIGURE 7. Blade of saw is passed through holes in metal
and fastened to the frame next to the handle

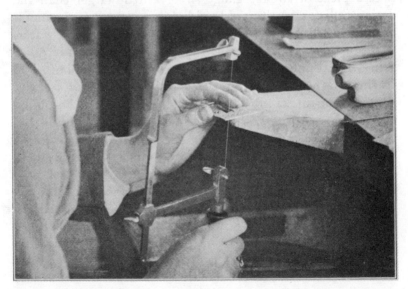

FIGURE 8. Correct position of frame for sawing

FIGURES 9 AND 10. Sawing with an up and down motion of the saw frame

of metal and the other end of the saw is securely fastened
(fig. 7). The tracing should be kept on the top side of the
metal. The saw is given an up and down motion cutting on
the downward stroke (figs. 8, 9, 10). A little practice in the
use of the saw in this way will soon enable the beginner to

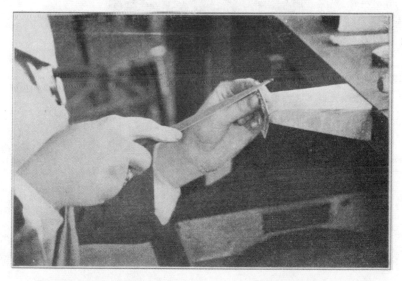

FIGURE 11. Truing up the edges of the work with a half-round file

do creditable work. After learning to control the saw the lines in the design are followed as closely as possible, being very careful not to cut into the line. After all the interior openings have been sawed out, the outline of the brooch is followed in the same way. An assorted set of 5½″ needle files is now necessary to true up the rough edges left by the saw. The half-round file is useful although there are times when other shapes will be needed (fig. 11). When all of the details have been carefully trued up with the files, the tracing may be removed by soaking in water for a minute or two and, when this has been done, the sharp edges of the openings may be removed by holding the file at an angle and going over the edges rather lightly. A strip of very fine emery cloth No. 000 may be used to finish the piercings. A large flat file is used to true up the outline of the brooch if it is regular in outline as fig. 5A.

A convenient way to keep a
collection of stones

BROOCHES

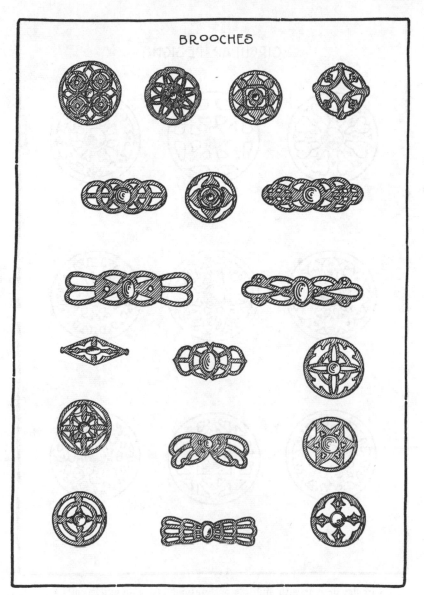

Perforated designs for elliptical and circular brooches

CIRCULAR DESIGNS

Circular designs with multiple perforations prove an opportunity for acquiring precision and accuracy. Suggestive designs for Problem 2

CHAPTER 4

Pierced Brooches With Stones

A B C

FIGURE 12. Silver pierced brooches showing variations between openings and metal

PROBLEM 2. We will leave problem 1 at this point and take up problem 2 which is to be a repetition of problem 1 except that it has a stone set in the center of the brooch (fig. 12). The piercing is done in the same way as in problem 1. When we have carried this to the point where we left problem 1 we next take up the making of a setting to hold the stone. This setting is called a bezel and is made of a strip of No. 24 or 26 gauge metal about one-eighth of an inch wide and long enough to go around the base of the stone. The ends are filed square and, with a pair of pliers, it is shaped around the base of the stone till the ends make a perfect union. The ends are then held in place by a piece of fine iron binding wire. The next step is to solder the ends together.

THE SOLDERING PROCESS

A borax slate, a piece of borum junk, a small soft hair brush and a piece of silver solder will be necessary to start (page 24, fig. 13). A little water is placed in the slate and the borum junk is ground in the water until it becomes milky. A fluid flux for hard soldering may be used in place of the borum junk if desired. The more care exercised in keeping

FIGURE 13. Borax slate, borum junk, and borax brush

borax and work clean, the more successful the results will be. Now take the bezel and with a small brush, coat the parts to be soldered, being careful to use no more borax than is necessary. Solder may be obtained in sheets any thickness, but No. 26 or 28 gauge is suitable for most purposes. It is cut in small pieces as shown in fig. 14.

First, scrape the sheet of solder with a scraper on both sides at the place about to be cut; second, make short parallel cuts evenly distant and about the same length. Now hold the solder between thumb and second finger with the first in front of cut edge of solder. Next, cut at right angles to set of cuts already made. This releases the solder and it will lay on the finger which keeps it from flying about. This is continued until the required amount of solder is cut.

METHOD OF CUTTING SOLDER

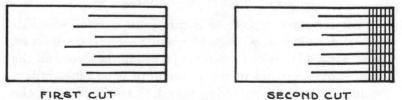

FIRST CUT   SECOND CUT

FIGURE 14. Method of cutting solder the easy way

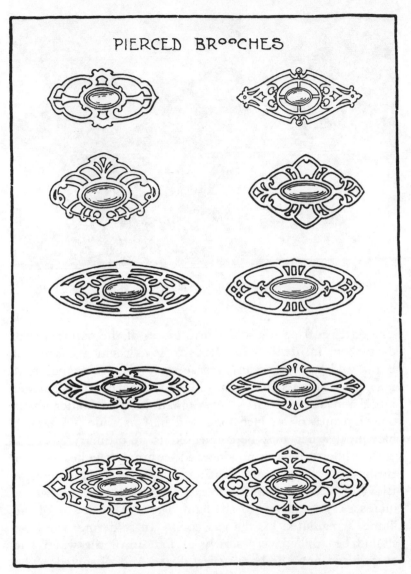

PIERCED BROOCHES

Designs for pierced elliptical brooches with stones, Problem 2

FIGURE 15. Soldering with mouth blowpipe, using poker to steady units

After cutting the solder into pieces of the required size, drop them into the borax slate to give them a coating of borax and to remove any grease or foreign substance that may have adhered to them. Place the bezel on a charcoal block and apply to the joint a small piece of solder about one-sixteenth of an inch long and half as wide. A mouth blowpipe, which may be connected to an ordinary gas cock with rubber tubing, is now needed to supply the heat—after turning on the gas and lighting, it is placed in the mouth. Blowing into the tube dilutes the gas with the air which increases the intensity of the flame (fig. 15). The size of the flame is regulated by the gas cock. In soldering, the heat should be applied very slowly at first until the water has evaporated and the borax crystallized and dissolved. The flame may then be applied more directly and the bezel brought to the soldering heat. If the heat is applied too quickly it will throw off the solder, and if heated hotter than necessary it is liable to melt or burn the parts being soldered, so the process demands very close attention from the start.

Instead of using a mouth blowpipe, a foot bellows and blow-torch may be used. This type of equipment is satisfactory for the more advanced student. After allowing the bezel to cool, remove the wire. If the binding wire should become soldered to the silver, which often happens, it can easily be pulled off with a pair of pliers. Copper or brass wire will not do for binding purposes. The bezel is now pickled or cleaned.

The Pickling Process

The solution called pickle is made of one part of sulphuric acid to eight parts of water. This solution may be used cold but is more effective if used hot. When used hot a copper pickle pan is necessary (fig. 16). The pickle is kept in a pickle pitcher (fig. 17). The object is placed in the pickle pan with enough pickle to cover it, then held over a gas burner and allowed to come to a boiling heat. The pickle is then poured back into the pickle pitcher and the object rinsed in clear water and dried in clean sawdust.

After pickling the bezel, the joint is filed inside and out to remove any surplus solder. It is then placed over an oval arbor and tapped lightly with a wooden, horn or rawhide mallet to make it perfectly oval. These types of mallets are used to prevent stretching. It may be that, when the stone

Figure 17. Pitcher for keeping pickling solution

Figure 16. Copper pickle pan

is tried in the bezel, the bezel is a little small; if such is the case, it can be stretched by tapping it with a metal hammer while it is on the arbor. The bezel is now filed flat on one side only, using the 6″ flat file. This can be done by holding the file in the left hand, resting one end on the bench pin, and holding the bezel between the thumb and fingers of the right hand, rubbing it up and down the file. A burr will form on the edge of the bezel and should be removed either with a small file or a scraper.

We are now ready to solder the bezel to the brooch; but before soldering, to improve the appearance of the brooch, it may be modeled or domed a little. This can be done either on a block of lead about 2″ x 4″ x ⅜″ or on a sand pad (page 30, fig. 18). If the lead is used, a small depression is made first by using a punch that will give the desired result. A chasing hammer is used to strike the punch, but if a larger depression is wanted, the sand pad is used and a wooden mallet with a domed end.

Now place the bezel on the brooch exactly in the center and mark on the brooch close to the bezel with a scratch awl or a sharp-pointed tool. Next, with the scraper, scrape on the inside of this line, making a bright surface about $\frac{1}{16}$″ wide. Borax the edge of the bezel filed flat and the surface of the metal just scraped. Be sure the bezel is exactly centered and then bind the bezel to the brooch with wire. Place small pieces of solder on the inside of the bezel and, with the blowpipe, apply heat as before, although this time care must be exercised to heat the larger piece first. When the bottom piece has been heated, the flame is directed over the work till the solder outside of the bezel is brought to the fusing point. Again, care must be exercised not to concentrate the flame on the seam of the bezel; the work should be turned so that the seam is away from the direction in which the flame is applied. After the solder has fused and the joint nicely flushed, the flame is quickly removed; and, after it has cooled, the wire is taken off and the piece of work pickled to remove the borax.

Silver brooches and flat surfaces set with semiprecious stones

FIGURE 18. Lead block and sand pad for doming flat metal

We are now ready to apply the joint and catch at the back. Both problems, Nos. 1 and 2, may be prepared and soldered at the same time. The joint and catch may be made by hand or a commercial one may be used. As this part of the problem is not important we will use the commercial one. On close examination of these two pieces, it will be found that they have slight burrs along the edges that turn over; these must be filed off in order to leave a perfectly flat surface. Scrape the places on the brooch where these are to be soldered. The joint is always placed on the right while the catch is placed on the left with the opening facing down when worn. They should be placed as close to the edge as possible. If the brooch is very much domed, the joint must be modified slightly. This is done by bending down on the part upon which the pin tongue is to rest. The joint and catch are set in place slightly above center, and a piece of solder is placed next to each. It is always advisable, when soldering catches and joints, to prop work up from charcoal block so that the flame can be directed under the brooch. When soldering these, the flame can be directed under the brooch and the flame should be applied very gradually. After the moisture in the borax has evaporated, the flame can be directed under the brooch so that it may become heated

FIGURE 19. Flat graver, shellac stick, and stone setting tool

first. If the flame were directed on top, the small pieces would heat before the larger and the solder would flow upon the catch or joint. For this reason both parts should be brought to the soldering point at the same time. The flame should be directed from the side opposite that on which the solder is placed. This will draw the solder toward the flame, hence in under the catch and the joint. This is easily done by directing the flame under the brooch until it is hot, then over it. When cool, the brooch should be thoroughly pickled.

SETTING THE STONE

After the joint and catch have been soldered in place and the brooch has been pickled and cleaned, preparations are made for setting the stone. In the first place, we must provide a way to hold the brooch firmly while the stone is being set. To do this, take a file handle and a circular block of wood, 2½ inches in diameter and ¾ inches thick, and fasten together as shown above (fig. 19.) On this, place dry orange shellac and melt it with the flame from the blow-pipe (fig. 20). Repeat this operation until there is about one-

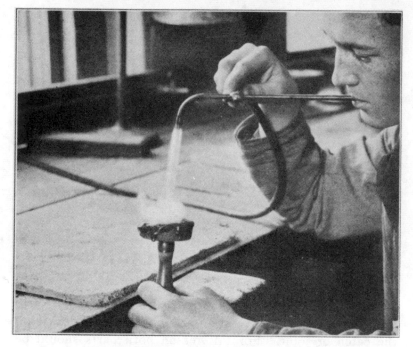

FIGURE 20. Melting dry orange shellac on the circular plinth block

quarter of an inch of the shellac on the top of the block. While it is still soft, press the brooch into the shellac until the upper part of the brooch has a firm bearing. The shellac is allowed to harden, and this takes but a few minutes. This holds the brooch firmly while the stone is being set.

The bezel is now filed down to the proper height (which is determined by the height of the stone), leaving just enough metal to cover the edge of the stone and to hold it firmly in place. The stone is next put in place and the bezel burnished over the edge. This is done by a small tool with a square end called a pusher. With this tool the setting is pushed toward the stone (page 33, fig. 21), first at the four points corresponding to the ends of the diameters. This is repeated at the intervening spaces until all parts of the setting touch the stone. A tool called a burnisher may be

Figure 21. Setting the stone with stone setting tool

Figure 22. Finishing the top edges of bezel with flat graver

Effective designs produced by drilling

used to rub or burnish the bezel perfectly smooth. A smooth file will finish the sides of the bezel and a No. 40 engraving tool is used to finish the top edge (page 33, fig. 22).

The shellac is now warmed a little with the blowpipe and the brooch lifted from the block with the tweezers. Care must be taken not to heat the stone, as semiprecious stones will discolor or burn if heated. When the brooch is taken from the shellac block, some of the shellac will adhere to it. This is removed by placing the brooch in a small dish and covering it with alcohol for a few minutes. The polishing and final finishing is done next and then the pin tongue is inserted in the joint. It is often necessary to open the joint a little, and this can easily be done with the chain pliers. After the pin tongue is in place, the sides of the joint are pressed together with the pliers. If the pin is too long it can be cut off with the shears and repointed. The point should project a little beyond the catch.

The above illustrations show how the drill may be used to produce effective results in the pierced brooch.

Flat wire edges give completeness to the design

CHAPTER 5

Brooches With Wire Edges

PROBLEM 3. To add to the interest of this problem a wire may be soldered to the edge of the brooch (as illustrated above) when the edge is regular in outline. The wire may be rectangular, round or oval. To get the length needed, the wire is placed next to the edge of the brooch and bent around it. It is cut a little longer than necessary at first and then filed to the exact length, butted well together and soldered. The ends can be made to stay in place while being soldered by springing one end by the other. Next, file surplus solder from the joint. This wire band should fit the brooch very snugly so that no space is left between the wire and edge of the brooch. If wire is too tight, it can be stretched by tapping it lightly with a steel hammer when placed on a round mandrel or arbor. Scrape wire bright on the inside and coat with borax. Now place it around the brooch so that the edge is flush with the back side of the brooch. Place small pieces of solder on the back of the brooch next to the wire at intervals of about one-half inch. The solder is placed on the back in preference to the front so that any superfluous solder can be filed off. When soldering, make sure that the solder flows all around. If it does not, apply more borax to solder and try again. The wire should project a very little above the surface of the brooch—about

FIGURE 23. Pierced brooches show design effect in the openings

one thirty-second of an inch. If it projects more than this amount, file and make sure that it is uniform in height. If the wire projects beyond the surface on the back it must be filed flush with the back. The wire should be free from sharp edges, and should feel smooth to the touch after it has been filed. Rub with a piece of fine emery cloth. If a round or oval wire is used it may be placed on the face of the brooch instead of on the edge as shown above, fig. 23. It will be noticed in these illustrations that the file has been used to make serrations at intervals along the wire to relieve

Brooches set with stones showing different effects in thick
and thin bands of metal

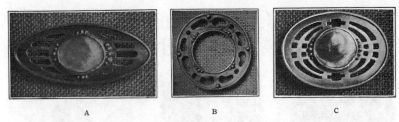

A   B   C

Figure 24. Variations of one motif in circular and elliptical brooches

the plainness of the edge and add interest. When the wire is applied in this way it should be carefully shaped and fitted to the edge of the brooch and held in place during the soldering with wire carried around the brooch as described when soldering the bezel.

Problem 4. To add still more interest to the brooch, in addition to the wire soldered to the edge described in problem 3, we can apply small shot varying in size as shown in fig. 24. These shot are made by taking round wire (No. 20 gauge) and cutting it in lengths to give the required size. These small pieces of wire are placed on the charcoal block and, after being coated with borax, are heated to the melting point. This causes them to roll up into the shot. When enough of these have been made they are spaced as desired and soldered in place. A small piece of solder is placed between each two shot. All other soldered joints should be protected with yellow ochre while this soldering is being done. After soldering the shot in place, the brooch is pickled and finished as already described. Fig. 24B has a rectangular wire soldered about the inside as well as the outside.

CHAPTER 6

Brooches, Carved and Ornaments Applied

Brooches of interlacing patterns of design produced with files and gravers

PROBLEM 5. The above illustrations show brooches or pins where the effect of interlacing has been obtained by a little carving. In this problem it is necessary to have the metal a little heavier or thicker than that used in the preceding problems. It should be not less than No. 18 gauge and in cases where considerable relief is desired No. 16 would not be too heavy. After making a tracing from the design, the tracing is glued, as before, to a piece of silver the required size and thickness. Next, take a scratch awl and follow the lines of the design, scratching through the tracing onto the metal, in order to have the design permanently traced on the metal. This operation must be carefully performed or the character of the design will be lost. The openings and outlines are pierced as previously described and trued up with the files. The interlacing effect is obtained by using the No. 40 graver to cut away the metal at points where one band or line goes under another. The shellac stick (page 31, fig. 19), is used to hold the piece of metal while it is being carved. After the carving has been done the rough parts are smoothed over with the files. In fig. 25B the whole design was filed or carried out in such a way as to give a modeled or rounded effect. The veins in the leaves, fig. 25C, were made with a three-cornered file. The flat wire was soldered around the outside (fig. 25B)

A   B   C

FIGURE 25. Brooches made by sawing and carving with few flat gravers

after the carving had been done. As a rule it is better to solder the bezel in place after the carving is completed.

In fig. 25 the carving is a little more difficult and requires two or three additional gravers, a No. 38 flat for getting into small spaces and No. 11 round for the curved parts of the design. In figs. 25B and C the background is cut away leaving the ornament in relief. It will be noticed that these brooches are domed, a thing which should be done before the bezel is soldered in place.

PROBLEM 6. In problem 6 the decoration is applied to the surface. Fig. 26 shows brooches where spirals of wire combined with shot have been used every effectively. A piece of No. 22 gauge metal is used for the back. With the compasses describe a circle the required size then saw and file to the line. Fig. 26C has a twisted wire about the edge. This is made by taking a piece of No. 24 gauge wire long enough so that when it is doubled it will give the length required to go around the brooch. After doubling the wire, place the cut ends in the vise and, with a nail or anything that will serve the purpose, twist the wire as shown on page 85, fig. 14. After twisting it from one end to the other, remove it from the vise, coat it with borax and place it on the charcoal block, page 85, fig. 15. Put three or four small pieces of solder at equal distances along the wire and heat to the soldering point, allowing the solder to run along the wire. This is done to hold the strands together so that they will not separate when cut. Although only two strands of wire

B

A

C

FIGURE 26. Button pins and elliptical brooch in appliqué,
using scrolls and leaves

were used in fig. 26C, any number can be used, the twisting being done in the same way. After the wire has been twisted and soldered, it is bent around an arbor to give it the circular form and cut the right size. The ends are soldered together as described in problem 3˙and, after truing it up on the arbor, it is placed on the metal forming the background of the brooch and soldered in place.

Several small pieces of solder should be placed about the inside of the wire equal distances apart. The bezel should be made and soldered in place as described in problem 2. The coil of wire shown about the bezel is made by coiling a piece of No. 30 gauge wire around a small arbor as shown on page 64, fig. P. This may also be done by putting the arbor in a lathe or in a hand drill. After the coil has been made, it is bent around the bezel to get the length and then the ends are soldered. It can also be soldered in place about the bezel at the same time if a little care is exercised.

The eight spirals are next made to fit between the coiled wire and the twisted wire at the outside edge. Take a piece of No. 30 gauge wire and cut eight pieces about 2½ inches long. Now fasten one end of a piece of wire in a pin vise and bend over at right angles. The vise is turned with the left hand while the wire is held with the thumb and first finger of the right hand. The vise is turned enough times to give the required number of turns in the spiral. It is then opened and the end of the wire held in the vise is cut off

Silver brooches of fancy wire with plain surface

close to the spiral. The spirals are then fitted in place and any extra length on the outside end is cut off. The eight spirals may all be soldered in place at the same time. After using the borax on all parts, several very small pieces of solder should be placed on and about the edge of each spiral. If the heat is applied gradually and the entire brooch brought to the soldering point at the same time, satisfactory results may be expected. The bezel and twisted wire on the edge should be protected with yellow ochre. When the soldering has been done the brooch is pickled. The shot as shown are now made and soldered in place. The ones forming the center of the spiral are flattened a little on the bottom. If one works carefully all of the shot may be soldered at once. The joint and catch are now soldered at the back and, after the final pickling, the stone is set and the brooch polished.

Fig. 26A differs from fig. 26C in that a beaded wire is used next to the bezel and next to the flat wire around the outside of the brooch, and a small round wire is soldered on the inside of the beaded wire. The three wires give an interesting finish to the edge. In using a combination of wires in this way, much depends on the relation one wire bears to the other regarding size and shape. On page 40, fig. 26B, the

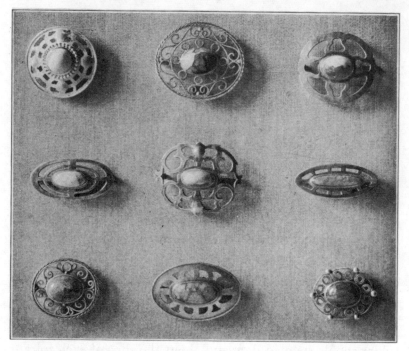

Brooches in silver executed in flat wire scrolls and by piercing

decoration is obtained by applying four small pieces of metal in the shape of leaves. These are connected with a piece of wire in the form of a stem, and a few shot suggesting berries. The only thing new in this illustration is the leaves which are cut out of No. 24 gauge metal and shaped up from the back with dapping punches on a block of lead (page 30, fig. 18). After they are shaped up they are filed off flat on the back and then, by using a three-cornered file, a vein or midrib is suggested on the face of the leaf. In this particular case a square wire was used for the stems. When the leaves, stems and shot are all made, they are put in place and all soldered at the same time.

BROOCHES IN WIRE

Wire brooch designs in delicate patterns

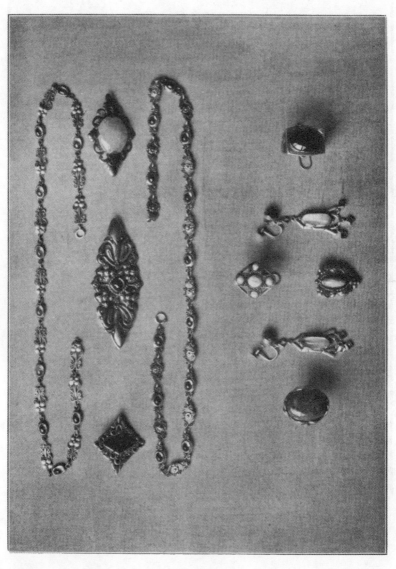

Jewelry ensemble carried through with a similar motif

Display of jewelry

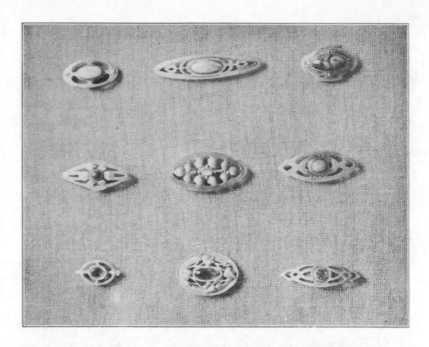

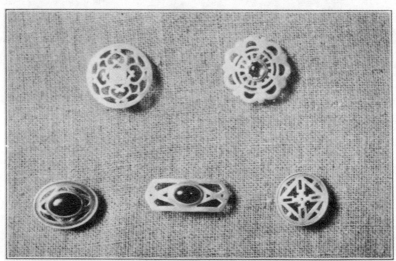

Brooches

CHAPTER 7

Brooches Made of Wire

FIGURE 27
Turquoise silver
pendant made
with flat wire

PROBLEM 7. In describing this problem the pendant (fig. 27) is used to illustrate because of its simple outline and few details. When the student is able to do the wire work illustrated in this figure and do it well, he will be able to produce more complicated pieces for most of the pieces of jewelry made up of wire are simply repetitions of different units. In this, as in most cases, a stone is the central feature around which is a wire design. We will take a cabochon cut stone. In this particular problem a turquoise matrix was used. The next step is to make a box or setting for the stone to rest in; this is done by making a bezel, using No. 26 gauge metal as described in problem 2. When the bezel has been made and shaped to fit the stone, it is soldered to a piece of metal the same thickness and just a little larger than the bezel. After the soldering is done and the box is pickled, the metal outside of the bezel is cut away. Cut with the saw just a little outside of the bezel and then file flush with the bezel. We are now ready to use the wire which, for this problem, will be rectangular, No. 15 x 22 (.057 x .025) gauge. It will be noticed that this design (fig. 27) is composed of three pieces of wire with scrolls at one end varying a little in size, and these three are repeated on each side of the stone. To make a good scroll is not easy, and considerable practice on the part of the student will be required. One must first come to an appreciation of the scroll through the drawing or design work, so it will be assumed that this most important lesson has been learned.

Wire and all metals when purchased may be had in the pliable or soft state. For our purpose here it is desirable to

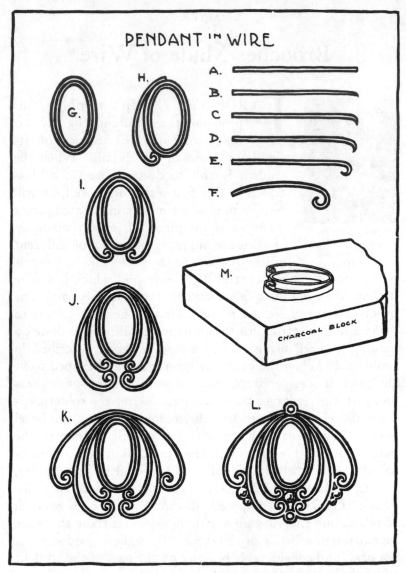

Progressive steps for making a pendant with flat wire, Problem 7

A   B   C

FIGURE 28. Flat wire in round, involute scrolls, and circles feature
new possibilities—note beaded wire edges

have the wire soft so it will easily yield to making scrolls. Metal that has been subjected to bending or pounding becomes tough. It can be softened by placing it on a charcoal block or an appropriate annealing tray and subjecting it to a flame till it comes to a red heat. The process is called annealing.

Take a piece of wire the size mentioned on page 45 and about one and one-eighth inches long and point one end with the file (page 46, figs. A and B). Now, with the round-nose pliers, hold the wire at the extreme end and by two or three turns with the pliers the scroll is started (fig. C). The pliers are then moved back a little and another turn is made as at fig. D and so on till it is shaped as at fig. E. Now take the round-nose pliers in the left hand and with the chain pliers in the right hand the scroll is completed (fig. F). Holding the tools and wire in this manner enables the student to produce a scroll with an unbroken line from the beginning. As stated before, this little operation will have to be repeated many times before satisfactory results are obtained, but when mastered, the most intricate design can be produced. Now to return to page 46, we will make the two scrolls that appear next to the bezel. After they are made and cut the right length they are soldered in place as at H and I. At the top, a part of the thickness of the wire is filed away to make the scroll appear to grow out of the setting; otherwise, when the other two scrolls are applied, it would be very heavy at this point. The next two scrolls are then made and soldered in place as the first two were (fig. J). The scrolls may be held in place while being soldered by using short pieces of iron wire placed next to the work and pressed into the charcoal block. While soldering a problem like this it is very important that the work rest on a level surface, so the charcoal block should be faced off from time to time, either with a large flat file or with a board covered with sandpaper kept at hand for the purpose. The middle scrolls are reduced at the top as the first two were and the outside ones are made and soldered in place as at fig. K. The last two are also filed a little at the top. After pickling, the piece of work is faced off at the back by placing it on the flat file and moving it back and forth a few times, holding it with the fingers of the right hand. If the soldered joints are irregular on the front side of the piece of work they may be filed a little with the flat file, keeping the safety edge next to the bezel to prevent reducing the thickness of the bezel. The shot as shown in the illustration are made and soldered in place. The rest of the parts of the pendant will be described under pendants.

Fig. 28 and fig. 29 can now be worked out being to a certain extent a repetition of the problem illustrated on page 46. In each of these figures, after the bezel is made for the stone, the outside frame is made and the other parts worked in between. In fig. 28B, after making the bezel and the outside frame, the inside is made of a series of circles or small rings of uniform size. These are made by taking a piece of wire the required size and coiling it over an arbor of the right size. This coil is then sawed apart, giving us the required rings. These are then placed on a surface plate and by tapping each one lightly, the ends are brought in line, or it may be done with the chain pliers, holding a pair in each hand. All the rings are placed on the charcoal block and are all soldered at once. After pickling, the joints are trued up with the file. The bezel is now placed in the center of the charcoal block and the frame outside of it. If the rings are made the right size, they can now be dropped into place and, after all parts are carefully adjusted and boraxed and a piece of solder placed over each point of contact, the whole

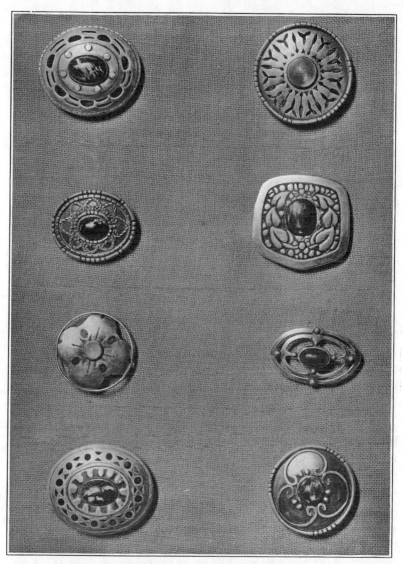

Silver brooches in piercing, carving, appliqué, and embossing

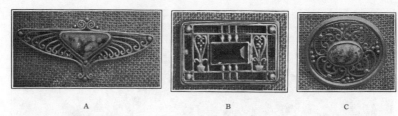

Figure 29. Brooches in contrasting contours made with flat wire

is soldered. After pickling, the front and back are faced off, using the flat file. A little more life may be given this piece by doming it as the pierced brooch was domed.

Fig. 29B differs from those just described in that a faceted cut stone is used and in that a large part of the brooch is made up of straight lines, requiring more accurate work. At first we must make what is called a shoulder bezel. Where the stone is transparent and cut as the illustration shows, the back of the setting must be left open so that the bezel is made with a shoulder on which the stone rests. To make the bezel in this way two strips of No. 24 gauge metal are needed about 3 inches long, one ¼-inch wide and the other ⅛-inch wide. These two strips are first soldered together. Before soldering, the two surfaces coming together should be cleansed or scraped bright and then coated with borax; and, after placing one over the other, they are bound with wire to hold them in place. Several pieces of solder are then placed at intervals along the edge and the two are soldered together. This gives us a strip of metal with a shoulder from which the bezel is made. Next make the outside frame, being sure that the opposite sides are equal and the angles right angles. The rectangle should be the same proportion as the stone. The next step is to solder the two bars that run from end to end. The ends of these strips should be filed squarely to make sure of a good joint. Now solder the vertical set of wires. Care should be taken always to have right angles, and the student should avoid using too much solder. In working with the shortest pieces of wire they can be handled by holding them in the flat-nose pliers. The student will save time in working out this problem if like operations on like pieces are done at the same time. The short pieces should all be soldered at the same time. In placing the wire, the student will find it helpful if he devises some method of holding the brooch firmly on the charcoal block. Short pieces of wire will serve the purpose as described in the preceding chapter. When soldering several pieces at the same time the student will get good results if a fairly large flame with a good mixture of air is used; in other words, a soft flame. When soldering the two strips that hold the bezel they should be placed so that the bezel will fit tightly. The bezel should be dropped in place to make sure of a tight fit before attempting to solder.

Now make two pieces like flower pots as shown (fig. 29B) of about 20 gauge metal and solder them in place. From the same rectangular wire make four scrolls to fit in place, and solder. Add the two smaller pieces and solder them. Now solder in the short vertical piece. This should be filed wedge-shaped at the bottom end to make a good fit. The four shot are made and first soldered together upon the charcoal block and then soldered in place. If the group of shot does not fit, the vertical wire can be filed a little until it does fit. The bezel is now put in place and soldered at each end after which shot are made to fit next to the bezel at the top and bottom and at the four corners of the brooch. All the shot should be soldered at the same time. To avoid unsoldering joints already soldered it is advisable to coat them with moist yellow ochre.

The outside of the brooch now looks very weak in design. To overcome this the brooch is soldered to a piece of flat stock of about 20 gauge. This piece should be larger than the brooch by about $\frac{1}{16}$ of an inch all around. The center is first sawed out so that the inside dimensions of the rectangle are equal to the inside dimensions of the outer rectangle of the brooch. The brooch is then soldered to this piece.

BROOCHES IN WIRE

Silver brooches of assembled wires, requiring numerous solderings

A   B   C

FIGURE 30. Round and flat wires gracefully combined with simple leaves

A piece of 26 gauge fancy wire, either twisted or beaded, is soldered in the corner next to the rectangular wire and upon the flat piece just soldered, adding much to the finish of the edge. Now solder catch and joint, pickle, set stone and polish.

PROBLEM 8. In fig. 30 natural elements have been introduced in the form of leaves and flowers. In fig. 30A the bezel is made as described in problem 7. Then two frames are made of round wire, one larger than the other and soldered together, with shot forming the point of contact. The leaves and flowers are made from No. 24 gauge flat stock. After cutting them the required shape with the saw they are placed on the lead block and are dapped up with the dapping tools. The outlines are finished with the file and the little stems which are made of small round wire are soldered to them at the back of the leaf. The stems are bent to fit and, after all the parts are fitted in place, the whole is boraxed and small pieces of solder placed at each point of contact and soldered.

In fig. 30B the work is much the same as in the preceding figure. The leaves are made in the same way and soldered to the stem, first a stem with three leaves and then one with one leaf. In this figure four small stones will be noticed at the ends of the long and short diameters of the brooch.

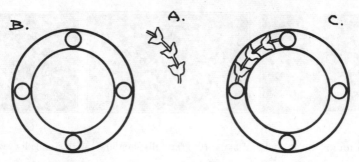

FIGURE 31.   Simple steps combining geometric and leaf forms

In fig. 31 the leaves are made as follows: Lay out the entire design on a piece of No. 24 gauge metal, being very careful in the drawing of the leaves. Use a No. 0000 saw to cut to the outline of the leaves. When this is done, turn the metal over, place on a lead block and, with very small punches, model the leaves as shown. In this case the leaves and stem are all in one piece and when filed up and cut apart appear as at fig. 31A. The settings are now made for the four stones. A piece of rectangular wire is used for the inside and outside rims. After making the rims, the settings are soldered in place as at fig. 31B and then the leaves are fitted and soldered in place (fig. 31C). Each leaf should come in contact with both the outside and inside rim.

CHAPTER 8

Brooches, Chased and in Repoussé

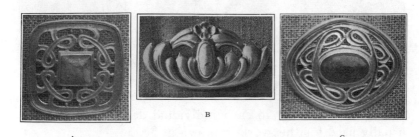

A   B   C

FIGURE 32. Brooches of natural forms and interlacing designs produced with a few chasing tools

PROBLEM 9. Fig. 32 shows brooches produced by the repoussé or embossing process. The principle is the same as modeling in clay or wax, the only difference being that metal is used as the material and different tools are employed. In this, as in clay or wax work, the object is to bring certain parts of the design into relief. To do this with metal, the work must be placed on a substance that gives some resistance and yet allows each blow of the hammer or tool to make an impression. The substance commonly used for this purpose has the following composition in the proportions given:

Black pitch	1 lb.
Tallow	3 teaspoonfuls
Plaster of paris	½ cup

The pitch is put in a dish, placed over a gas plate and melted. The tallow is then added and the plaster stirred in gradually, the whole being well mixed. It is then poured into the pitch pot and allowed to cool. When used in hot weather, more plaster will be needed. The pitch pot, on page 57, is hemispherical in shape, made of cast iron about ½-inch thick. This, when placed on a chaser's pad, may be turned at any angle. The tools necessary for this work may be made

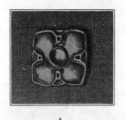

A   B   C

FIGURE 33. Nature-like designs produced by repoussé and doming

as needed according to each individual design. A hammer usually used for this work is shown in fig. 34.

We are now ready to take up the problem. In fig. 33A No. 24 gauge metal is used. The design is carefully drawn or transferred on the metal and then lightly scratched with a scratch awl to make the drawing more permanent. The pitch is now slightly warmed on the surface and the metal placed on it. After it has cooled, we are ready to carry out the design, which, in this case, is to be in repoussé.

First take a small narrow tool, hold it as shown in fig. 34, and carefully follow the outline of the design. By using the chasing hammer and striking the tool with a repeated number of uniform light blows, a channel is made in the metal and, when we reverse the piece of work, we shall find that a line has been raised around the outline of the brooch as in the illustration. It will also be noticed that the four petals or leaves radiating from the center are to be raised slightly. This is done with a larger tool slightly convex. After the tooling is completed, we are ready to remove the work from the pitch. Take the blowpipe and warm the metal slightly, just enough to soften the pitch, and then the work can be lifted with a pair of tweezers. Some of the pitch will adhere to the work, but it is easily removed by rubbing over it, while it is warm, with a cloth dampened with kerosene. After it is cleaned, if we find that the embossing is not quite satisfactory, it can be placed on the pitch again and worked over to improve it.

Figure 34. Pitch pot, engraver's pad, and tools used to chase
or emboss a design in metal

When the tooling is satisfactory, a bezel is made for
the stone and soldered in place. The stone in this case is a
moonstone. Figs. 32B and C are done as fig. 32A except
that the tool was used on the face as well as on the back.
The lines that form the midribs or veins of the leaves are
made by using the tool on the front side of the brooch. The
tooling done on the face of the work is called chasing.
Fig. 32B and the pendant on page 79 are examples that
show the technique and results obtainable. These results are
realized, however, only after long and continued practice.
Figs. 32A and C, also fig. 35 show problems carried out
in interlacing. The design is laid out on the metal as previously described and, after placing the work on the pitch, it
is chased. The entire outline of the design is followed first
with a rather pointed or V-shaped tool, sometimes called a

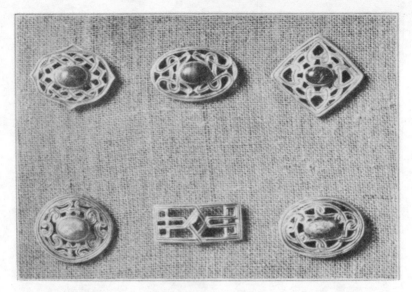

FIGURE 35. Interlacing effects easily made by the chasing process

liner. Then a larger tool of the required width is used to go over the interlaced parts. After the chasing is done, the open parts are cut out with the saw and the edges finished with the file. In this problem it is better to bevel the edge a little, rather than have it vertical. After the chasing, sawing and filing are completed, the bezel is made and soldered in place, also the joint and catch at the back. The stone is then set and the brooch polished.

Stylized pierced pin

PROBLEM 10. A brooch with several stones may be carried out as shown in figs. 36, 37 and 38. A piece of No. 18 gauge metal is used for this problem. The design is first carefully drawn on the metal and then pierced with the saw. A piece of work of this nature requires very careful filing after the sawing is done. The settings for the stones are made differently from those previously described. Before making the small triangular piercing, next to the large stone, make an opening in the center of the piece of metal the shape of the large stone but one quarter of an inch less in diameter. Then place it over an arbor and turn up the metal from the inside about the edge of this opening by hammering and stretching. This forms the bezel (fig. 36). The small piercings next to the bezel may now be drawn, sawed and filed into shape (fig. 37). Now place the metal front-side down on the lead block and dap up the leaves about the edge with a good-sized dapping tool. Drill a hole in the center of each leaf, using a drill about one-sixteenth of an inch less in diameter than the size of the stone. As the stones vary in size, each one will have to be fitted separately. After making the openings for the stones about the right size, a shoulder is cut around each opening to make a seat for the stone. As cabochon stones with flat backs are used in this particular instance, the

FIGURE 36. The first step is the embossing, the second is fine piercing

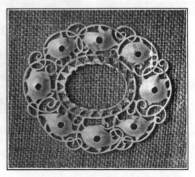

FIGURE 37. The piercings next to the bezel and the openings in the leaves are prepared to receive the several stones (as fig. 38)

shoulder is cut flat. When each one of the small stones has been carefully fitted and numbered, the setting for the large stone is carried farther. From a piece of flat stock about No. 24 gauge and three-sixteenths of an inch wide, make a ring large enough to fit inside of the opening for the large stone. As it is necessary to have a good snug fit, the ring can be made just a little small at first and stretched to fit. This ring is soldered in place, keeping it about one-sixteenth of an inch below the top of the edge forming the bezel. This makes the shoulder on which the stone rests. The joint and catch are now soldered in place and the stones are set after the brooch is polished. The large stone is set as previously described after placing it on the shellac stick. The small ones are set by using a small half-round engraving tool, turning the metal over the edge of the stone at four points. Upon close examination of fig. 38, the marks of the engraving tool may be seen. In this type of setting the stone must fit the opening perfectly.

Figure 38. Opal and moonstones set in lace-like design produced by fine piercings

CHAPTER 9

Pendant

Silver pendant set with inexpensive shell pearls

PROBLEM 11, as illustrated above. The first things necessary for this problem are the two stones that form the central feature of the pendant. The ones used in the illustration are pieces of shell pearl. This kind of pearl is inexpensive and looks very well when set in silver. Having the pieces of pearl or whatever may be chosen for the central unit, a box setting is made for each piece. In making these settings, the bezel is first made for each stone from No. 24 gauge fine silver $\frac{1}{8}$ of an inch wide. After cutting the strip the right width it is bent around each piece of pearl to get the exact size. Mark at the point where it is to be cut, remove the pearl and cut on the mark. We now have the two bezels shown on page 62, A and B. Bind each of these bezels with the binding wire and solder the joints, C, D. One face of the bezel is next filed level and soldered to a piece of No. 22 gauge silver, E and F, which is to form the back of the setting. After soldering, the two settings should be pickled to remove the borax. Next saw around the bezel within $\frac{1}{32}$ of an inch of the soldered joint. The edges are then filed even with the bezel as shown at G and H.

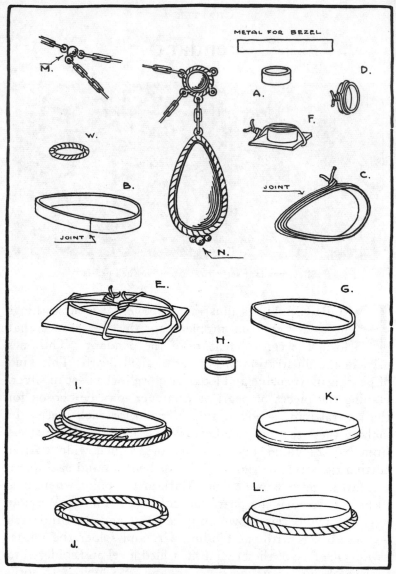

Sequence of steps for making a simple silver pendant, Problem 11

As the design calls for a twist about the settings, take a piece of No. 24 gauge silver wire twice as long as the distance around the settings, double it, place one end in the vise and twist. Plan to have enough wire to make the twist for both settings at the same time. After the twist is made and a little solder is run along the twisted wire, it is bent around each bezel to get the exact size, before it is cut (fig I). The cutting here should be done with the saw as it will leave the ends of the wire square and make a better joint when soldered. After the joints are soldered we have two rings, figs. J and W. The top of each bezel is next filed down to the right height and beveled to an edge as at K. The twisted rings are now placed over the bezels as at L and soldered in place. Care should be taken to have the twist come even with the back at all points. If the twist has been made to fit tightly it will stay in place while being soldered without the use of binding wire. In soldering this, several small pieces of solder should be placed along the twist, for the solder will not flow along the wire freely as it does not come in contact with the bezel at all points. Contrarily, the solder will flow up and around the wire instead of along the joint. The soldering should be watched quite closely at this time and the flame kept away as much as possible from the other soldered joints to prevent unsoldering.

We now make the five small shot that are shown in the design at M and N, page 62. To make these shot, first make a small hemispherical depression in the top of the charcoal block about $\frac{1}{4}$ of an inch in diameter and about $\frac{1}{8}$ of an inch deep, page 64, fig. O. Take a small piece of copper, 18 or 20 gauge, and file one end to a dome, hold it against the charcoal block and with two or three turns the depression is made. Care should be taken to give the depression a smooth surface. Now take a small piece of the scrap silver that was sawed from the edge of the bezel and place it on the charcoal block over the depression. With the blowpipe, heat the silver to the melting point and it will roll into the depression and take the shape of a ball. A little experiment-

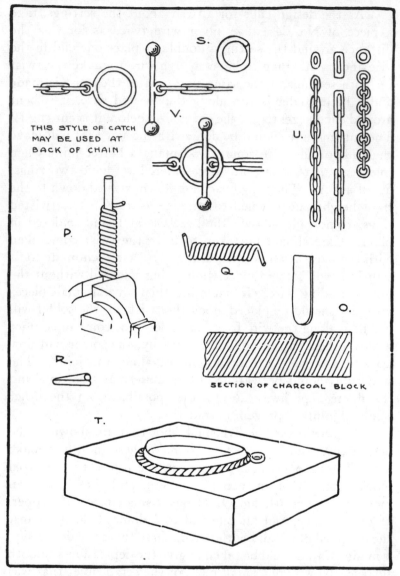

Making links for chain and plain catch, Problem 11

Various simple treatments of semiprecious stones for pendants

ing with different sizes of scrap metal will enable one to get just the size wanted. After making the five shot needed we next make the small rings that connect the chain with the bezels and with two of the balls. As there are twelve of these rings needed and as they are the same size, they can all be made at once. Take a small arbor about $\frac{1}{16}$ of an inch in diameter and fasten one end in the vise together with one end of a piece of No. 24 gauge silver wire. Holding the other end of the wire with a pair of pliers, coil it about the arbor until twelve or fifteen turns have been made (fig. P). Taking it out of the vise and slipping the coil from the arbor leaves it in the shape of a small spring, Q. Now with a fine saw, the rings are sawed apart. The rings are now as at R. Using the pliers, the ends are given a slight twist to bring them in line with each other. The rings are now soldered to the bezels and the shot. Before soldering, however, each ring should be filed a little flat, as at S, where it comes in contact with the bezel. The filing is done just a little to one side of the joint which has been left unsoldered so that it can be opened to receive the chain when ready to put together. The rings are so small that they should be held with the pliers while the filing is done. When the rings are ready, the bezel is placed on the charcoal block, fig. T, and the ring put in place. Coat the joint with light borax and place a small piece of solder over the joint. The flame from the blowpipe is next applied and the soldering is completed. The bezel that requires five rings and the one with three may be all soldered at the same time. If the borax used is too thick it will be difficult to keep the rings in place. The three shot are now soldered in place at the bottom of the large setting. When this is done all parts are pickled.

The stones are set as described in Chapter 4, page 23. The parts are next linked together with the chain. Those who desire can make the chain in the same way that the small rings are made. The shape of the link is determined by the shape of the arbor on which the wire is wound. This arbor may be round, oval, or rectangular, and make chains as shown on page 64, fig. U. A commercial catch may be used at the back as shown in the illustration or one may be made as shown on page 64, fig. V. The chain and settings may be oxidized a little to give them a gray finish which looks well with the pearl.

Wire pendant set with garnets and pearls

A   B   C

FIGURE 39. Lavalieres in flat scroll wire set with turquoise and tourmaline

WIRE PENDANT

PROBLEM 12, fig. 39A. This pendant is made of rectangular wire. First make the bezel, solder it to a flat piece about 22 gauge and saw out the back. File the outside flush with the bezel as on page 68, fig. A. Now make the two scrolls next to the bezel as fig. B. In making the second scroll from the first, care must be exercised to have them exactly the same size; this can be done by juxtaposition or by making one scroll then straightening it out to determine the exact length required for each scroll. Two pieces of wire are then cut to size and made into scrolls. When they look exactly the same and completed they are soldered next to the bezel. The setting may be held firmly upon the charcoal block by using small pieces of iron wire about one inch long. These are inserted vertically through the opening of the bezel and next to it down into the charcoal. After soldering these two scrolls, file them at the top as at fig. C. Make the two other scrolls in the same way and solder them. Again file the ends of the wires at the top of the pendant as was done in fig. C. The two small scrolls in fig. E are made and soldered in the usual way. Before soldering, be sure that the lower scroll touches all four of the other scrolls. Next,

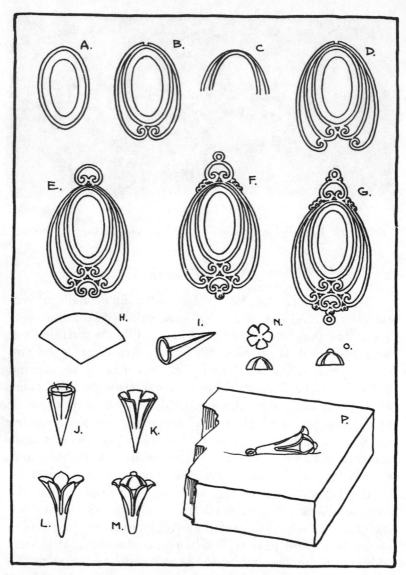

The 16 steps in making the wire pendant

Varied pendants made of flat wire

solder on the shot and then the link at the top of the pendant as in fig. F. Solder the two shots and the link at the bottom as in fig. G. To make the drop, saw out a pattern for a cone of 22 gauge metal as fig. H. Bring the edges together with pliers as fig. I. Place the cone over the end of a piece of steel that has been pointed on an emery wheel and, with a steel hammer, bring the edges together until they touch. Solder at the seam, using plenty of solder. Stand the cone on the base, place solder on the apex and solder again. The solder should fill the opening at the apex so that when it is filed it will finish to a point. Divide the circumference of the base into five equal parts as in fig. J, then saw down these points to about one-half the depth of the cone as shown by the same figure. Next spread each part with pliers as shown by fig. K and file them to shape as fig. L. Make a form large enough to fit into this bell-shaped drop, fig. N. A small shot is soldered on top as fig. O. The drop is then imbedded vertically into the charcoal block with the apex down and the form soldered in place as fig. M. The apex is next filed squarely and then slightly rounded. We are now ready to solder on the link. Imbed the drop again into the charcoal block in a horizontal position, and solder the link as shown in this illustration on page 68, fig. P. The link, however, is to be left open so that the open part is not soldered to the drop.

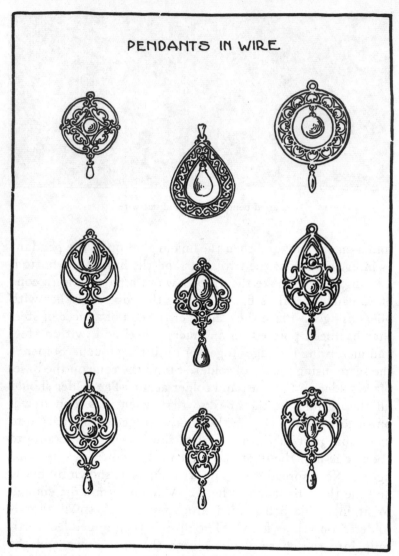

PENDANTS IN WIRE

The involute curve in designs produced in flat wire makes delicate pendants

The slide is made as described on page 76, inserted, and then soldered. After the drop is attached to the pendant the work is pickled and the stone set in the usual way. The pendant is then finished by polishing and coloring.

PROBLEM 13, fig. 39B. In this problem a rectangular wire is used. Either the lower or the upper part of the pendant may be made first. A bezel for the triangular stone is made and soldered to a flat piece of silver, which is then filed close to the bezel as on page 73, fig. A. The back is sawed out leaving enough metal to support the stone. The back of the bezel is always cut away when transparent stones are used. The outside shape of the pendant is made like the design and to conform to the bezel as fig. C. The ends at the top are soldered and filed as in fig. D, then it is soldered to the bezel as in fig. C. The student should solder each scroll in place as made, as each piece determines the exact size of the next piece. Make the scroll above the stone and solder as in fig. D. Now proceed to make the two smaller scrolls on each side of the stone by making the larger ones first. When the four are made to fit snugly, solder all at the same time. The three shot over the first scroll are made separately and soldered in place; the same is done with the others as shown in fig. F. All the shot and the link at the top in the same figure may be soldered simultaneously if the ability of the students warrants. The pieces of silver for the shot should be cut from wire since it is easier to control the sizes. The experienced worker usually has a small bottle full of shot, previously made, from which he selects the required sizes. The wire at the bottom of the pendant as marked by N is filed partly away.

Make a bezel for the elliptical stone at the top with an open back. From the same rectangular wire make four scrolls of the same size and solder to the bezel just made as fig. G. To get them exactly the same size the student should make one, then it should be straightened to get the exact length of the wire. Four pieces of this length are cut and made into scrolls. If all four cannot be soldered at once, at least two should be soldered, one on each side of the bezel, then the other two are soldered in the same way. Next make two ellipses of the same wire as figs. H and I as large as indicated by the ellipse in fig. L. Center fig. G on the ellipse fig. H and mark by the scrolls. This will determine where they must be cut. Care should be exercised not to make them too short and to keep their curvature. The same is done with the smaller ellipse I. The first four pieces of fig. J are soldered in place as at fig. L, then the smaller pieces in fig. K. The links which are made of round wire are then soldered as at fig. M. The slide is made in the usual way; it is soldered when in place and then the work is pickled. All parts are carefully examined to make sure that the pieces are securely soldered. The bezels are next prepared for setting the stones. When they have been set, the two parts are connected with a link made of round wire. The link is closed with the pliers and left unsoldered.

PROBLEM 14, fig. 40. Choose a stone of about the same proportions as the one in the photograph and make a box setting for it as previously described. Saw out the back, leaving about $\frac{1}{16}$ inch shoulder for the stone to rest on as fig. A, page 75. Now take a piece of 20 gauge flat silver large enough for this problem and draw on the design as at fig. B. Place the bezel on this metal and mark its position as shown by the ellipse in the same figure.

Saw out the design leaving an opening for the bezel just large enough to receive it snugly as fig. C. Take a piece of rectangular wire and make a rectangle for the outside of the pendant as fig. D. Connect figs. C and D by soldering two metal strips between them as fig E. These strips should be made of the same wire as that used for fig. D. On a piece of 22 gauge flat silver draw the shapes of the flowers. The drawing of the flower should be made a little larger than is actually required as it is to assume part of a hemispherical form when finished. Saw out the flower as on page 76, fig. 41U. Take

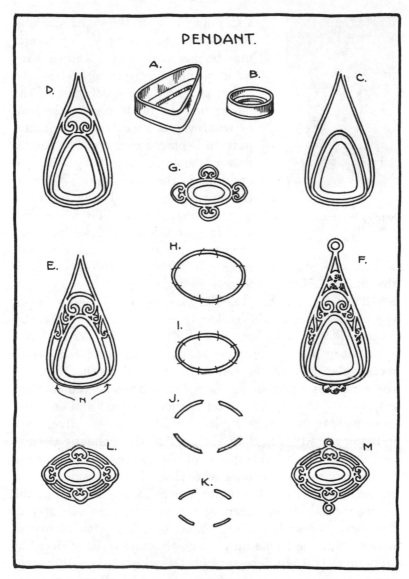

PENDANT.

Steps for making a rectangular wire pendant in two parts, Problem 13

FIGURE 40. Shell pearl happily combined with scroll, straight line and florets

a dapping tool of the right size and shape the flowers as fig. V. The metal may be placed on pitch, lead or hard wood while this is being done. An impression of the general form of the flower may be made first in the lead or whatever is used, then the metal pattern is placed over it. The square flowers shown on page 76, fig. Z, 1, 2, 3, are done in the same way. When all the flowers are shaped they are ready to receive the shot. There are five shot in each flower. Make four shot the same size as fig. W, place a small piece of solder on top and apply the flame. Now place one shot on top of the four and solder again, fig. X. Do likewise for the others. When the clusters are made, pickle them and solder one group in each flower as in figs. Y and Z3. The flowers are then adjusted in place as on page 75, fig. F, and soldered. With rectangular wire of the same size as used for fig. D make the scrolls as those in fig. G. These are soldered in their respective places. The bezel is then inserted and soldered as in fig. H. Now take a piece of 20 gauge flat silver that is larger on all sides than the part of the pendant already completed. From this piece of 20 gauge metal, make a frame having an opening the size of the inside of the rectangle D, as fig. I. Solder the pendant, already made, on top of this frame keeping the margin even all around. The two pieces should be bound together with plenty of wire so that the frame may touch the part to be soldered at all points. It is not necessary for the wire to pass completely across the pendant in binding. This will allow a piece of 20 gauge copper a little smaller than the opening of the frame to be placed under the pendant while soldering. The piece of metal if covered lightly with yellow ochre will prevent it from being soldered to other parts. The purpose of this

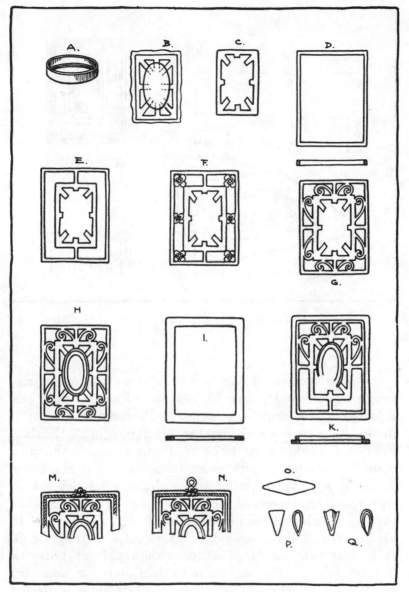

The A, B, C of making the rectangular silver pendant, Problem 14

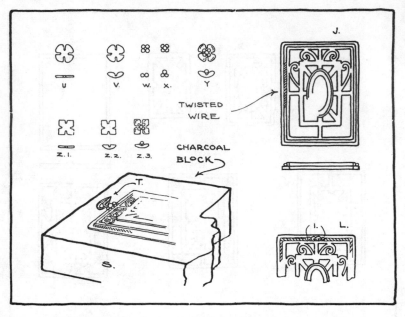

FIGURE 41. The final steps in the making of the rectangular
silver pendant (see page 75)

metal is to keep the flowers and bezel from sagging. A rectangle similar to D, page 75, is made of twisted wire and soldered on the frame as at fig. 41J. Part of this wire, at 1, in fig. L, is removed with a graver to make room for the shot. Four shot are then soldered on the frame as seen in the same figure. The remaining three are soldered next to the frame as at fig. M, page 75, after which the ring for the slide is soldered to the largest of the three shot as fig. N. The slide through which the chain passes is made of a flat piece of 18 gauge silver. The pattern is first made on the metal as fig. O. It is next bent as fig. P either with a pair of pliers or over an arbor. The surface is filed in places as indicated by fig. Q to relieve the flatness. The slide is passed through the link at the top of the pendant as fig. 41S and soldered at T. The pendant is now pickled after which the stone is set.

Suggestions for silver pendants: *at the left*, a Chrysoprase pendant; *upper center*, Tourmaline; *lower center*, Butterfly design; and *right*, flat wire scrolls giving lace-like pattern

FIGURE 42
Pendants made by
piercing, appliqué,
and enameling

PROBLEM 15, fig. 42. For this pendant use a piece of 22 gauge silver 2″ x 1½″. The design is first made and transferred to the silver on the side that is to be the back of the pendant. After scratching the design on the silver, it is placed upon the pitch block face down and the leaves are slightly shaped or domed with a dapping tool. The whole pendant can be slightly domed, to give it a little more character. The piercing is done after the doming and shaping of the leaves. The finish on the outer edge of this pendant is made of twisted wire which gives the appearance of being plaited. A piece of 26 gauge wire is doubled and the ends are placed in the vise and twisted to the right. Another piece is twisted to the left in the same way. The two, when placed side by side and soldered, give a plaited effect. They may be held in place, while being soldered, by coiling fine binding wire around them. The wire is now bent into an ellipse which should be made small enough to leave a margin on the pierced metal and the ends soldered. It is next soldered on top of the pendant. The solder should be placed at frequent intervals on the inside of the wire. If the wire cannot be made to touch at all points on the flat piece, solder wherever

it does touch, then press down on the elevated places when cool and solder again. The shot and ring at the top are soldered as in the previous problem and the slide is made in the usual way.

PROBLEM 16, fig. 43. No. 20 gauge metal is used for this problem. The design is drawn on or transferred to the metal which is then placed on the pitch block (fig. 44). A small chasing or lining tool is used to trace the outline of all the parts of the design (page 57, fig. 34). The metal is then taken from the pitch and turned face down. Chasing tools and punches are used here and there to give the desired relief. The metal is again turned over and worked from the face of the pendant. The details of each flower, leaf and stem are brought out with the various chasing tools, although considerable practice will be

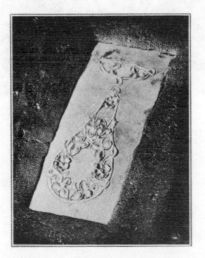

FIGURE 43. Problem 16

FIGURE 44

necessary before satisfactory results are obtained. The saw
is used to cut away the background, leaving the parts as
shown in fig. 45. The settings are made to fit the stones and
soldered in place. In this problem all of the settings are open
back as shown in fig. 46. This figure also shows the way the
leaves and flowers look from the back where they have been
dapped up. The various parts of the pendant are linked
together with the chain and the stones set.

FIGURES 45 AND 46. Front and back views of the pierced and
chased naturalistic design

Pendants

Wire pendant with bell drops

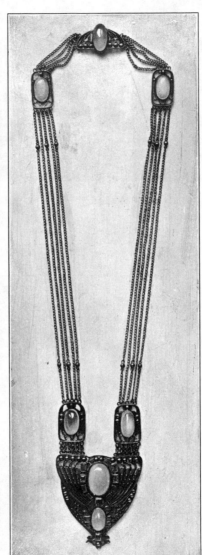

Pendants

CHAPTER 10

Finger Ring

PIERCED RING

PROBLEM 17, fig. 47. The size of the ring must first be determined. This is found by using the ring sizes or by measuring with a narrow strip of paper around the finger on which the ring is to be worn. When this strip of paper is straightened out it will give the length of the metal needed for the ring. Usually a precious or semiprecious stone is made the central feature of the ring. As the size

FIGURE 47

of the stone will determine the width of the ring at the top, it is necessary to know this at the beginning. A variety of methods are used in fastening the stone to the ring, which are called settings. The simplest form, known as a box setting, is employed in the ring illustrated. Not knowing the length of the metal needed and the size of the stone and the kind of setting to be used, a drawing of the design as on page 83, fig. 1, is necessary. Then make a careful tracing, fig. 2, from the drawing and glue it to the surface of the metal, fig. 3, A and B. For the ring here illustrated, No. 18 gauge sterling silver is used, 2¾″ long and $\frac{9}{16}$″ wide. After the glue is thoroughly dry it will hold the tracing firmly in place. A small drill, No. 60, is used to make openings through which the metal saw is placed. For this problem a No. 00 saw is needed as the openings are quite small in places. Saw as closely to the line as possible, being careful not to cut into it. After the openings are sawed out (fig. 4), file them true with the needle files. A square and a knife edge are needed to finish the small openings. Next cut the metal the required length and file the ends square. When the filing is completed and all rough edges are removed it is bent into

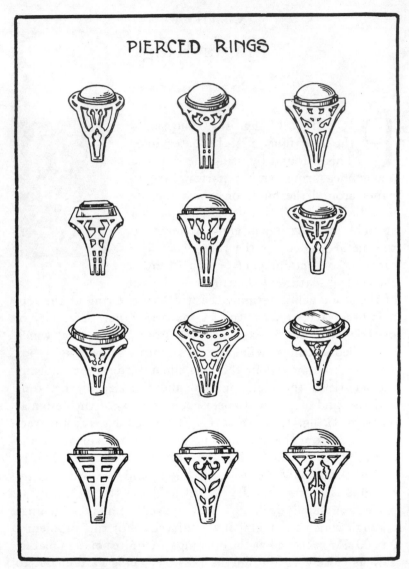

PIERCED RINGS

Pierced ring designs, a challenge to able designing, Problem 17

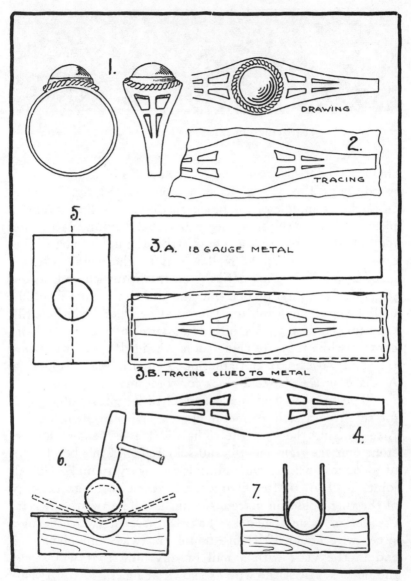

Various steps in making the pierced ring in silver, Problem 17

Pierced silver rings set with cabochon stones

shape. To do this, bore a hole with a ¾″ bit into a piece of wood about 2″ x 3″ x 2″ as shown on page 83, fig. 5. Saw through the middle of the block on the dotted line. Take a piece of ⅝″ dowel or a ring arbor and having placed the metal over the block as at fig. 6, strike the upper part of the dowel or arbor with the mallet, driving the metal into the form as at fig. 7. Then striking on the upturned ends as on page 85, fig. 8, first on one side and then on the other, gradually bring them nearer together as at fig. 9, and continue till they touch. Use a piece of binding wire to hold the ends in contact while they are being soldered, fig. 10. After coating the joint with borax and applying a small piece of solder at A, place on the charcoal block for soldering.

The bezel is next made from No. 24 gauge silver and for this ring a strip of metal 1¼″ x ¼″ is needed, fig. 11. After cutting the strip the right width it is bent to fit the stone, cut the right length, and soldered. As this bezel is to fit a convex surface, some filing is necessary to make a good joint, fig. 12A. After fitting the bezel perfectly to the top of the ring, solder in place as at fig. 13. The twist shown in the design is next made. Take a piece of No. 24 gauge silver wire about 12″ long, double it twice and place one end in the vise; with a nail or anything that will serve the purpose, twist the wire as shown at fig. 14. After twisting it from one end to the other, remove it from the vise, coat it with borax and place it on the charcoal block (fig. 15). Put three or four small pieces of solder at equal distances along the wire and heat to the soldering point, allowing the

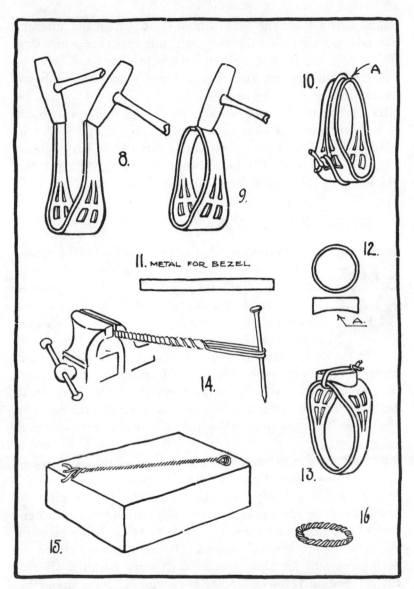

11. METAL FOR BEZEL

Continuation of steps in making the first ring in silver, Problem 17

solder to run along the wire. This is done to hold the different strands together so that they will not separate when cut. When this has been done bend the wire about the bezel to get the required size and then cut and solder the ends together, making a ring as at fig. 16. A little filing may be necessary at the joint to work the ends together. Now place it over the bezel as shown on page 83, fig. 1, and solder in place. The ring is next pickled to clean off the borax about the soldered joints. The bezel is filed to the right height, the thickness of the edge reduced and the stone set.

WIRE RING

FIGURE 48

PROBLEM 18, fig. 48. To make the finger ring in this problem use a circular stone of about ¼″ diameter and some No. 14 gauge wire.

First determine the size of the ring as described in Problem 17. Take two equal lengths of the wire as A, B, on page 87 and bend into circles, as C, D. Next file ends flat and solder. Place these two rings on an arbor and use a rawhide or wooden mallet to make them circular. Care must be taken not to stretch either ring as they should be kept the same size. Next place the rings side by side with soldered joints together as shown at E and bind with wire at places indicated by F. While soldering be careful that the solder does not flow beyond points 1 and 2.

We are now ready to make the bezel. Take a piece of bezel silver No. 24 gauge a little longer than the circumference of the stone and about ¼″ wide as at G, also a piece of the same length but ⅛″ wide as H. Scrape one surface on each piece and file the edges of each strip parallel. Borax the scraped surfaces and place the strip ⅛″ wide upon the strip ¼″ wide with scraped surfaces facing each other (fig. 1). Bind with wire and make sure that edges 1–2, and 3–4 are parallel. Now place small pieces of solder along 3–4 and apply heat from the direction indicated by the arrow in

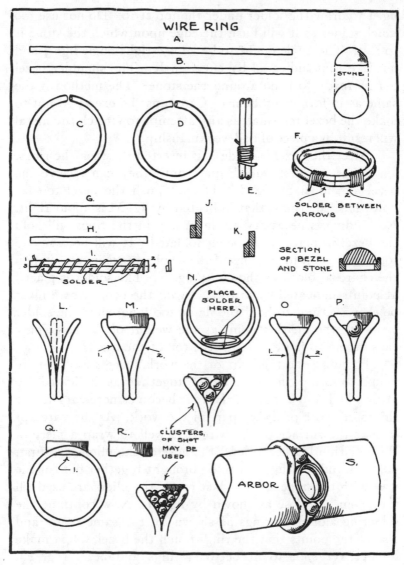

Simple steps produce a ring as Figure 48, Problem 18

fig. I to draw the solder under the top strip. Do not use too much solder as it will flush the edge upon which the stone is to rest. The angle ought to be kept a right angle like J and not like that indicated by curve in K. The shoulder bezel is now ready to bend around the stone. The method is the same as in former problems. Care must be exercised not to make the bezel too small as any attempt to stretch the metal will result in a piece of bad workmanship.

After the bezel is made it is inserted between the rings. The rings are first pulled apart until they can receive the bezel as shown by fig. L. Do not push the bezel too far down into the rings; that indicated by fig. M is about right. No binding is necessary as the spring in the rings will hold the bezel in place while being soldered. It will be easier to solder the bezel to the rings if the whole ring is inverted upon the charcoal block as shown by fig. N. The solder is placed at points indicated by arrows. Again the utmost care must be exercised not to hold the flame too long while the solder comes to the melting point as the weight of the rings may cause them to fall even with the top of the bezel.

Having done this part of the work successfully, we are ready to bring the wire closer together as indicated by arrows at 1 and 2, fig. M. Here it becomes necessary to use the round-nose pliers for part of the work. As they are apt to mar the surface of the wire it is well to wrap a piece of cloth or thin leather around the nose of the pliers. At first, points 1 and 2 of fig. M can be brought together part of the way with the fingers. As a last resort the pliers are used till they come as close as shown by fig. O. Now continue the soldering along the rings as shown by the same figure and also at the points that the rings touch the bezel. Next make some silver shot to fit between rings and bezel (fig. P). Several shot may be used if desired. The shot should touch in three places; a small piece of solder is placed at each point of contact and then soldered. It is advisable to solder one shot at a time, unless a cluster is used and then they may be soldered together first.

Fig. Q shows that the bezel comes below the wire at 1. This will have to be filed off with the half-round file till it conforms to the ring as represented by fig. R. The ring is now ready to be cleaned and pickled. The stone is set in the usual way except that the work can be accomplished more easily if the ring is placed over an arbor as shown by fig. S. After the stone is set, the ring is polished and oxidized if desired.

FLAT RING WITH LEAVES APPLIED

PROBLEM 19, page 90. To make the ring as illustrated here take a piece of 20 gauge metal and mark out the pattern in the usual way. Next file to the drawing as fig. A and bend as shown in the previous problem on the ring. When it has been shaped and soldered at the joint as fig. B, make the bezel. The bezel should be made high enough to allow for filing as fig. C. It is then filed as fig. D to conform to the shape of the ring and then soldered as fig. E. In this ring the two wires 1, 2, in fig. F along the surface of the shank are 28 gauge. Two separate rings are made the size of the largest diameter of the ring as fig. G and bent as in fig. H, to conform to the contour of the shank. They are adjusted in place as in fig. F and soldered all around. If these rings are made to fit tightly it will require no binding. The leaves are made of 24 gauge silver; the drawing is first made on the metal and then it is sawed as fig. I. They are then dapped up in a lead block. The leaf is placed so that the drawing of the midrib is next to the lead. After it is slightly domed as fig. J, file the surface along the lines delineating the midrib as fig. K. The metal may also be removed with a graver. Having made the midrib on all the leaves, they are adjusted to the surface of the ring by bending with pliers or flattening where needed. Care should be taken that they touch the surface of the ring at all points. Next place two leaves on one side of the ring as in fig. L and apply small pieces of solder around the leaves. See that they are soldered at all

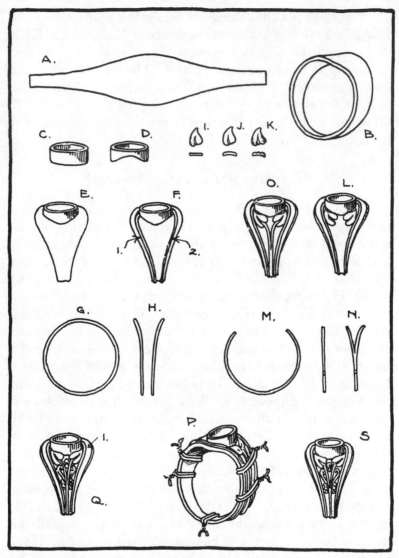

Steps in making a flat ring with leaf ornament, Problem 19

points. Having done the same with the other side it is ready for the stems. Take a piece of square wire about the same size as the round wire used for the rings in fig. G, and make a ring of the same diameter. Cut out a piece of this ring as in fig. M so that the wire when applied to the ring will reach from the leaves on one side to those on the other side. Slit the wire at each end and spread as in fig. N. Apply this wire as fig. O and bind as fig. P. The smaller pieces of wire and shot may now be made to fit. All the pieces on one side should be soldered at the same time. When the other side is completed, the ring is pickled and the small pieces just soldered are tested separately to make sure they are securely soldered. The margin at 1-Q is next filed narrower and to a slight chamfer as in fig. S. The bezel is then filed to the proper height to receive the stone. In setting the stone the ring may be held in a ring clamp or placed over an arbor to help keep its shape. When the stone is set it is finished by filing and polishing respectively. This ring is illustrated below.

Silver ring in leaf design gives
complete aesthetic satisfaction

FIGURE 49. Finger rings produced by piercing, chasing and carving
with engraving tools produce ruggedness of appearance

THE CARVED RING

PROBLEM 20, fig. 49. When the design is to be carried
out by carving as in this problem, the blank ring must first
be made and filed into shape as desired. The design is
sketched on the blank and held in the ring clamp as shown
in fig. 50, page 93. A variety of engraving tools, both round
and flat, are needed for the carving. The cutting is a slow
process and the tools have to be handled with complete control to avoid slipping. After the cutting is carried to the
desired point, small needle files of assorted shapes are used to
smooth up the work. Sometimes the ring is put on an arbor
and the lines are more clearly defined here and there by the
use of a chasing tool. The background may be matted in
the same way if desired.

Left, filed and carved; *center*, carved; *right*, file grooved

Rings in appliqué and carving

FIGURE 50. Taking out the background of the design with engraving
tool, Problem 20

(From left to right) Belcher, Gypsy and Tiffany settings

THE BELCHER SETTING

FIGURE 51

PROBLEM 21, fig. 51. To make this setting, a ring is first made of metal thick enough to take the depth of the stone to be used. (fig. 52A). After filing the blank into shape, use the center punch to start a hole for the drill. This hole should be on the top of the ring and in the center. The size of the drill used is determined by the size of the stone. The hole should be smaller than the diameter of the stone. A small round file is used to file the metal away in making the prongs. The six prongs or points in this setting require careful filing to have each one equal in size as well as to have the openings uniform. When most of the filing has been done, a burr which is similar to a drill (fig. 52D) is used to make a seat for the stone. These burrs are made in various sizes (page 95, fig. 53), so that one

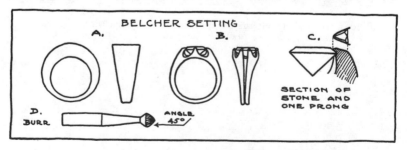

FIGURE 52. The making of the belcher setting, Problem 21

may be selected having the right diameter for the stone. After the seat has been made, the file is again used to remove more of the metal and to shape the ring as desired (fig. 52B).

FIGURE 53.   Assortment of Jewelers' burrs used in making seat for the stone.

While the ring is held in the ring clamp the stone is placed in position (fig. 54) to see if it fits. If it does not fit exactly so that the edge of the stone bears evenly all around the seat, a little of the metal may be removed with the graver where necessary (fig. 55). The stone is again put in position and when it rests so that it is level (fig. 56), it is ready to set. During the fitting process the stone is held with a small piece of wax. The setting tool is now taken and held as shown in fig. 57 and each of the prongs is pushed

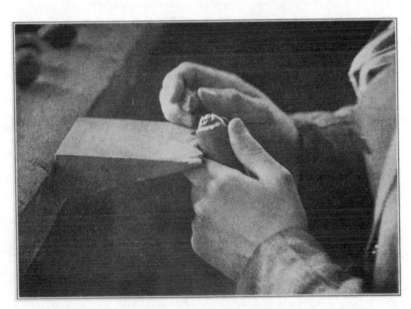

FIGURE 54. Trying faceted stone in a belcher setting for a good fit

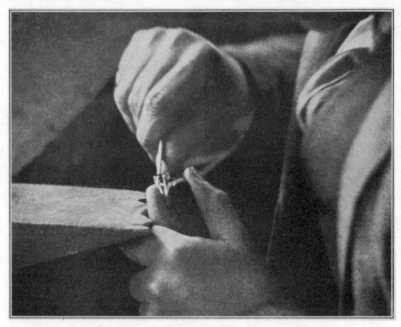

FIGURE 55. Cutting seat for stone with graver

FIGURE 56. Examining the stone to prove level position

FIGURE 57. Position of the setting tool against the prong while setting stone

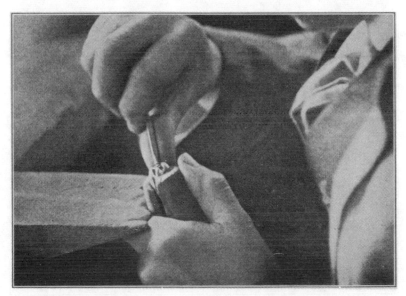

FIGURE 58. With setting tool in a more perpendicular position, the stone is made secure

FIGURE 59. Shaping the top of the prong with flat file

FIGURE 60. Bright cutting the prongs with flat graver

gradually over the stone. After pushing the first prong in place, the one opposite should be pushed next and so on with each of the other prongs. When the prongs have been

forced part way over the stone, the file is used to remove a little of the metal at the top of the prong so as to make it easier to force the point of the prong completely over. Holding the setting tool in a more perpendicular postion (fig. 58), the points are pushed over until the stone is held firmly in place. The file (fig. 59) is again used to shape the top of the prongs and then the flat graver (fig. 60) is used to cut the point as shown on page 94, fig. 52C. This is called bright cutting and completes the setting.

FIGURE 61
Tiffany ring

THE TIFFANY SETTING

PROBLEM 22, fig. 61. The Tiffany or prong setting is used mostly for setting diamonds or other transparent stones. A conical tube is first made of No. 18 gauge metal (fig. 62A). The height and diameter of this tube is determined by the height and diameter of the stone. The shank of the ring is made and the tube soldered in place (fig. 62C). The file is used to make the prongs (figs. 62B and D). The ring is imbedded in the shellac with only the setting exposed. Then

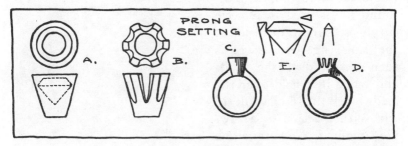

FIGURE 62. Tiffany or prong setting made in four simple steps, Problem 22

with the engraving tool the bearing or shoulder for the stone to rest on is cut (fig. 62E). The prongs are all adjusted with a pair of pliers so that the stone will fit tight. The stone is pressed down firmly until the edge rests evenly on the bearing of each prong. This leaves the ends of the prongs projecting above the edge of the stone. The next step is to push all these ends firmly over the edge of the stone (fig. 62E). When the prongs are all in their places they are trimmed to a point with the engraving tool. This is usually done by making a cut on either side of the point and one on the top, and is termed bright cutting the prongs.

THE GYPSY SETTING

PROBLEM 23. The Gypsy ring (fig. 63) is made by taking a piece of heavy metal long enough to make the required size and as thick as the stone to be used is deep. Lay out on the blank (page 101, fig. 64A) the long and short diameter and scratch lightly on the metal. Then with the saw and file shape the blank as shown at fig. 64B. After this is carefully shaped so that it is symmetrical, it is placed over the lead block (fig. 64C), and with the ring arbor it is turned up and the ends brought together for soldering. A generous piece of solder is wedged in between the ends (fig. 64D), and if carefully fitted when soldered, the ends will spring together and show very little of the solder. After the joint is soldered, the half-round file is used to remove surplus solder on the inside of the ring (fig. 64E). It is then placed over the arbor and while it is held over the lead block it is shaped up with either a lead or a raw-hide mallet. Now take the file and true up the edges on

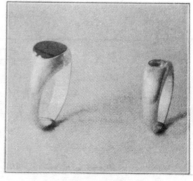

FIGURE 63

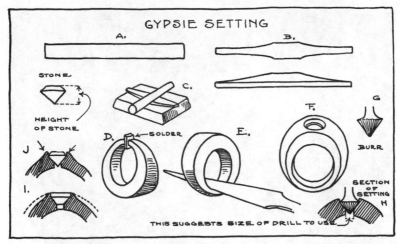

FIGURE 64. From ring blank to making ready for circular stone
in a gypsy setting, Problem 23

the outside, being careful to retain the lines that were
scratched on the blank at the beginning. After it is filed so
that it is symmetrical on either side of the long and short
diameter of the block, it is placed over the arbor and a small
depression is made at the intersection of these two lines using
the center punch. This depression is a beginning for the
drill which is used to make the hole at the top of the ring.
The ring is held in a clamp during the drilling or it may be
held in a vise and done with a hand drill. The size of the
drill should be determined by the size of the stone, and should
be much smaller than the greatest diameter of the stone
(fig. 64H). After this hole has been made the next step is to
take a burr (fig. 64G), and ream out the hole to the size of
the stone. If the burr is allowed to sink a little below the
surface of the top, it will form a seat or shoulder on which
the stone rests (fig. 64F). Up to this time the ring has been
flat with square corners, but it is now time to file it into the
desired shape by rounding the corners and removing some
of the metal at the top next to the setting (fig. 64I). After
the ring has been filed into shape and the file marks removed
by using fine emery paper, it is ready for the stone.

FIGURE 65. Reducing the metal around stone for streamline effect

In setting the stone the ring is held in the ring clamp (fig. 65). At first, make sure that there is a level shoulder or seat for the stone to rest on. The metal may be removed as needed with the engraving tool, and when everything is ready the stone is dropped into place. The pusher as described in Chapter 4, page 32, is used to force the metal over to the stone (page 101, fig. 64I). This is done at first at four points and then, after more of the metal has been removed with the file, the pusher is used again, and these operations are repeated until the metal has been completely pushed over and the stone held firmly in place. A little more filing is necessary to finish the setting and after using the graver to finish the edge next to the stone, the setting is completed. It is then polished and finished as desired.

Fig. 66 is worked much the same as Problem 23 except that the stone is cut to conform with the outline of the ring. In this ring the stone is oval in shape which requires a little different handling than with the circular one. A hole is

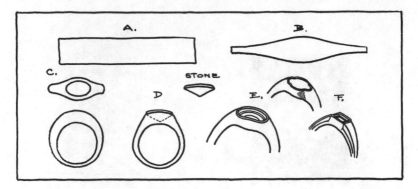

FIGURE 66. Making the gypsy setting for an oval and square stone

drilled the required size as before and then it is necessary to file the opening to fit the stone. The shoulder or seat must be cut entirely with the graver in this case, and as the stone is cut on the arc of a circle it makes the setting more difficult. The stone is set in the same way as in problem 23.

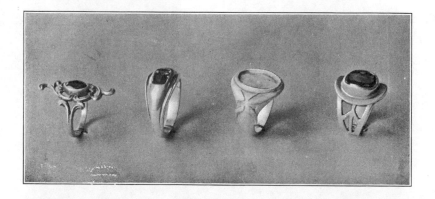

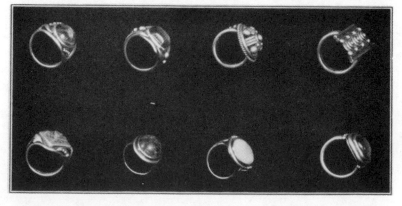

Rings in silver, in harmony with quality of stone, character of design
and type of setting

Silver rings ranging from the simple to the intricate designs,
and from the single stone to the cluster

Chapter 11

Chains

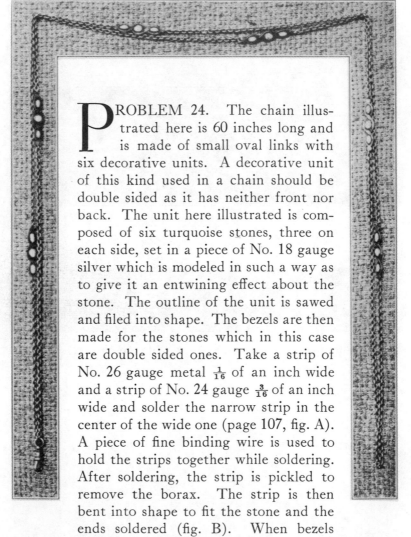

PROBLEM 24. The chain illustrated here is 60 inches long and is made of small oval links with six decorative units. A decorative unit of this kind used in a chain should be double sided as it has neither front nor back. The unit here illustrated is composed of six turquoise stones, three on each side, set in a piece of No. 18 gauge silver which is modeled in such a way as to give it an entwining effect about the stone. The outline of the unit is sawed and filed into shape. The bezels are then made for the stones which in this case are double sided ones. Take a strip of No. 26 gauge metal $\frac{1}{16}$ of an inch wide and a strip of No. 24 gauge $\frac{3}{16}$ of an inch wide and solder the narrow strip in the center of the wide one (page 107, fig. A). A piece of fine binding wire is used to hold the strips together while soldering. After soldering, the strip is pickled to remove the borax. The strip is then bent into shape to fit the stone and the ends soldered (fig. B). When bezels have been made for the 36 stones, holes are drilled in each of the units and the bezels are carefully fitted and num-

Chain designs

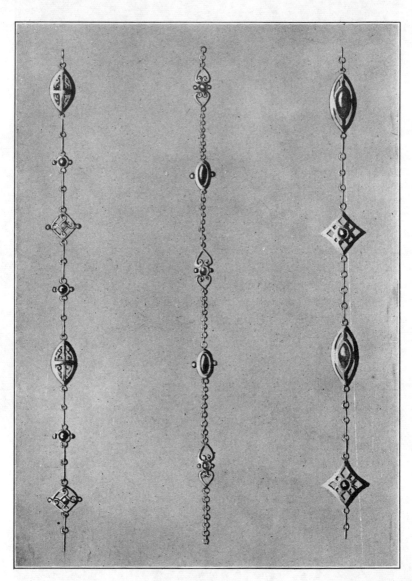

Chain designs

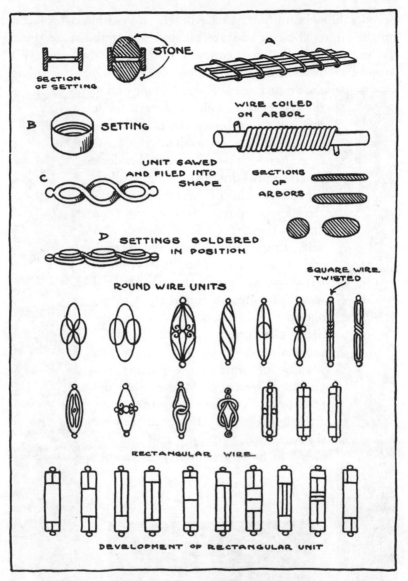

Making the double face and wire units for the long chain, Problem 24

bered. The six units with the bezels in position are placed
on the charcoal block and are all soldered at the same time.
To make the links that connect the units, wind the wire
around an arbor the shape and size desired to make a coil as
shown on page 107, fig. A. One end of
the arbor can be held in the vise while
the coiling is being done if only a
small number are needed. If a lathe
is at hand the coiling can be done
much more quickly. The coil is
slipped off the arbor and the links
are sawed apart. These are then
linked together and soldered. A
small ring or link is soldered to each
end of the unit. The illustration at
left shows a chain with units made of
wire. The illustration at right shows
one in which the units of wire have
been alternated with a bead of
tourmaline. Page 107 suggests a
variety of unit arrangements for
chains. The shape of the arbor determines the shape of the links,
although they may be made in many
shapes—oval, round, and oblong
ones are most frequently used.

Silver bracelet for girls

CHAPTER 12

Cuff Links and Cuff Buttons

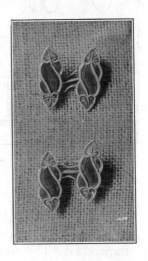

PROBLEM 25. The cuff link and cuff button is usually made up of three pieces, the button, stem and bean.

The button, if circular, is about $\frac{11}{16}''$ in diameter and if elliptical about $\frac{1}{2}''$ x $\frac{3}{4}''$; the bean may be spherical, hemispherical or bean shaped as in fig. 67E. If spherical or hemispherical it may be $\frac{5}{16}''$ diameter and if bean or lentil in shape it may be $\frac{5}{16}''$ x $\frac{7}{16}''$. The stem is usually a piece of round wire about $\frac{3}{4}''$ long and No. 8 gauge. The button which is the only part that gives chance for decoration may be worked out with a pierced, chased, etched, applied, or enameled design. If an enameled or etched design is chosen, the stock should be heavy; about 12 gauge. If a chased design is desired a piece of 24 gauge metal is suitable (fig. 67A). This thin piece is afterward domed (67B), the design executed, then soldered to a flat piece of 20 gauge (C). In all cases it is well to have the button slightly domed when finished. The superfluous metal is then sawed away (D). Assuming now that the button is complete, the next step is to make the bean. This can be made of 20 gauge metal in the shape of a sphere or hemisphere.

The stem can be made of No. 8 gauge round wire. Take a piece about $\frac{3}{4}''$ long and slit it longitudinally about $\frac{3}{4}$ its length (F), using a very fine saw blade. The stem is now ready to be soldered to the bean, but before doing the soldering it is necessary to make a small drill hole on the bean next to the place where the stem is to be soldered, to avoid combustion when soldering. A strong union of the

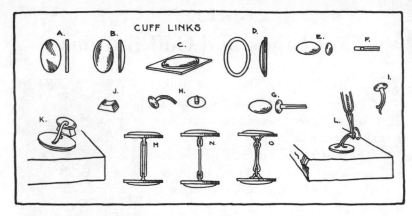

FIGURE 67

two pieces (G) should be secured by using plenty of solder. The stem is then curved with pliers or over an arbor with a mallet (H). The ends of the stem are then spread and shaped (I). The stem and bean can be soldered to the button by holding them with tweezers (L) or by making a metal support (J) to hold the bean in place (K). When soldering make sure to flush the joints to assure strength. Now the cuff link is ready to be pickled and then polished.

If enamel is to be used it is applied after all soldering has been completed. In this case an extra hard solder must be used to prevent joints becoming unsoldered in the enameling process. Before firing, the joints are heavily protected with yellow ochre.

CARVED CUFF LINKS

Gold brooches in black enamel using the champlevé process

CHAPTER 13

Enameling

THE art of enameling has been practiced from very early times, dating far back in history. Probably it is unknown when the practice commenced. Many of the early examples now to be seen in the British Museum date as far back as the tenth century B.C. Enamel in its simplest forms was in use among the Egyptians, Phoenicians, Assyrians, Greeks, Romans, and Etruscans, and is seen at its best in association with jewelers' and goldsmiths' work.

The Egyptians used a fine royal blue glaze on the small images of mummies which were placed in the tombs to be the servants of the dead in the next world, but its use upon metal to any great extent is doubtful.

In the early Greek work it is quite probable that the glass blowers and jewelers worked together. A ring in the British Museum with a band of glass about it gives evidence of this fact. Although there are many examples in the museums of Europe of work done up to the fourth century A.D., we know more about the art of enameling from then on.

It was about this time that the art was practiced by the Greeks at Byzantium and by the Celts in Ireland. The Greeks at Byzantium practiced what was termed cloisonné and the Celts the champlevé form of enameling, and for five centuries their work was unrivaled for its beauty. During the tenth century the art of the Byzantine enamelers began to decline and at the same time it sprang up in Western Europe.

About the fourteenth century it was carried from Constantinople across Asia to China by artificers who set up workshops on their way. Toward the end of the sixteenth century the art was carried from China into India and Japan.

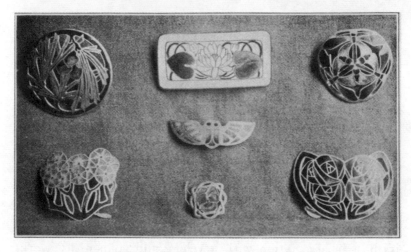

Brooches in champlevé, grisaille, and basse-taille enamels. This medium offers opportunity for color expression

The art was introduced into Europe by Theophano, a Byzantine princess who, when she married Otho II, brought with her enamelers from the East. Her interest in craftsmanship resulted in the art being practiced in Trives, Cologne, Maestricht and Verdun and probably found its way from these places to Paris. It was not until the twelfth century that the art was practiced at Limoges which was a Roman colony and was known for the quality of its goldsmiths' work. The prosperity of the place attracted Byzantine and Venetian craftsmen and during the thirteenth century an enormous quantity of work was turned out which was both good and bad. In the fourteenth century the art declined to such an extent that it went out of fashion altogether.

Toward the end of the fifteenth century, however, the art was revived again and Limoges started up her enameling ovens with renewed vigor, handing down to us priceless treasures of the enamelers' art. The best Limoges enamels come from such artists as the Penicauds, Courtey, Limosin, Raimond and Landin.

Enameling as a truly fine art again began to die in the 17th century and was not practiced to any extent till the middle of the 19th century. The names of Herkomer, Fisher, Varley and Stabler are associated with the best modern work.

ENAMEL POSSIBILITIES

With the use of enamel it is possible to reproduce the various play of colors in opals, in labradorite, the translucency of such stones as the agate and onyx and a brilliance of transparency equal to that of emeralds and rubies. It is made to last and if kept out of the ground and protected from actual rough usage it will suffer little deterioration. Nothing but burial in damp earth can impair it.

This peculiar gem-like quality, unlike anything else in art materials, gives it a peculiar charm. And when applied to objects in metal, it adds a great deal to their attractiveness and value. Good judgment, however, must be exercised in the amount of enamel used. In some articles, such as pieces of jewelry, little enamel should be used, thereby giving it the character of a gem. There are many objects to which enamel may be properly applied, such as scarf pins, cuff links, brooches, buckles, clasps, pendants, necklaces and earrings.

KINDS OF ENAMEL

There are three kinds of enamel: transparent, translucent, and opaque. The transparent reflects the color and surface of the metal, while the opaque gives color on the surface only. The translucent admits the light partially.

COMPOSITION OF ENAMEL

Enamel is composed of a flux combined with oxides of metals. The flux is composed of silica (powdered flint or sand) minimum which is red lead, nitrate or carbonate of

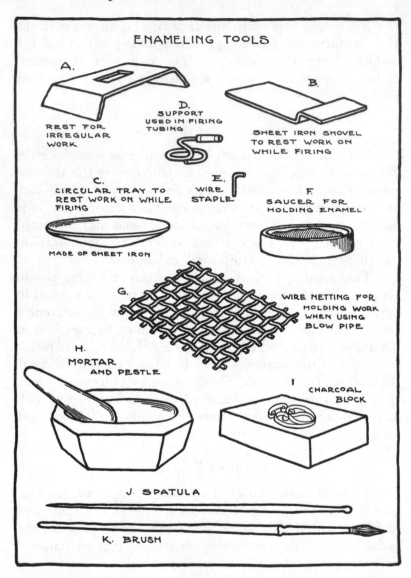

A few of the essential tools used in enameling

Grinding the enamel in mortar with pestle

soda, or potash, all melted together in a crucible until there are no bubbles left in it. This flux which is the base of all enamels is combined with different metallic oxides in various proportions. There is no limit to the range of color that can be produced except that vermilion and lemon-yellow cannot be obtained.

Transparent enamels are made opaque by adding oxide of tin and white arsenic. As the metallic oxides give the required colors, and as these colors are liable to change under various degrees of temperature, great skill and patience are necessary to determine the exact degree and the time of exposure which will insure the hue intended by the artist.

Because of the vast amount of knowledge and experience necessary to make enamel, the craftsman or jewelry worker will do well to leave that part of the art with the one who makes it his profession. There are difficulties enough in handling the enamel, after it is made, to tax the ability of the amateur to the limit.

GRINDING

The best hard enamel, mostly made in France, usually comes in thin cakes varying in size from two to six inches in diameter and about three-eighths of an inch thick, although it is sometimes made in lump and rod form. The cake or lump is first broken into small pieces with a hammer. One or two of the pieces are then broken up again until it is about as fine as coarse sand. If only a small quantity is wanted, it can be rolled up in a piece of heavy wrapping paper while it is being broken. The paper prevents it from flying about. After being broken it is placed in a porcelain mortar (see page 113), with water enough to cover it, and ground as fine as fine sand, with the pestle. For very small work or jewelry, it is ground much finer with the use of the agate mortar and pestle, see page 112, fig. H. The water is poured off and the enamel rinsed several times until all of the milky substance disappears. Unsatisfactory results often come from lack of care in washing the enamel. It is a good plan to have a dish to pour the washings into to save enamel that would be wasted. This waste enamel, as it is called, is used for counter enameling. After being washed, the enamel is removed from the mortar to a small saucer, by the use of a palette knife.

ENAMELS

There are seven methods or processes used in enameling, which are as follows: Cloisonné, Champlevé, Painted Grisaille, Basse-taille, Plique-à-Jour and Niello.

THE CLOISONNÉ

In the Cloisonné method the outline is all-important, and as this outline consists solely of the wire which encloses the various fields of color, its design must be simplified to the last degree.

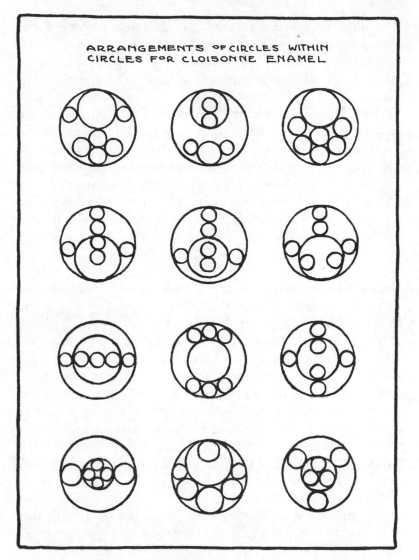

Arrangements of circles soldered on metal for cloisonné enameling

With its severe limitations, it demands at once a fine sense of color and the most careful drawing.

Cloisonné enamel is produced by setting· up cells or cloisons on the surface of the object or material to be decorated. This is done by bending flat or rectangular wire into the shapes called for in the outline of the design and then soldering these wire units on to the material which forms the background. The wire thus forms cells into which the enamel is placed and then melted or fused in the furnace.

At first a careful tracing is made for the design, giving all the lines that are to be in wire. This tracing is then placed on a charcoal block which has been faced off level with the use of a file. Now, using a small pair of pliers, the wire is bent into the shape of the design, fitting all of the lines on the tracing paper. These pieces of wire are then held in place by the use of small staples made of iron wire which are forced through the tracing into the charcoal block, pinning the cloison wire to the charcoal. After the design is completed and the parts all fitted together, the joints are coated with borax. Small pieces of solder are then applied to each joint and the whole is soldered with the use of the blowpipe flame. The paper tracing burns away during the soldering operation. After removing the iron wire staples, the wire design is pickled to remove the borax. The metal plate that is to form the background is next thoroughly cleaned and coated with borax. Now place the wire design on the plate and press it gently until it conforms with the surface of the plate. Small pieces of solder are placed at intervals along the wire forming the design and, after coating with borax and binding lightly with iron wire, it is placed in the furnace until the solder runs. Boil the plate out again in the pickle to remove all borax and thoroughly clean it. When this has been done it is ready to receive the enamel.

CHARGING. Assuming that the enamel has been ground to the required degree of fineness and carefully washed as previously described on page 114, a small quantity of each color to be used is placed in small porcelain saucers. If the

Applying the enamel with an improvised spatula

design is carried out in copper, a saucer of flux is necessary to start with. In order to retain the transparency of the enamel, a coating of flux must be applied and fired on before applying the colors. If silver or gold is used, the flux is not necessary. While the enamel is still wet, it is applied to the object with a metal tool called a spatula, which may be made from a piece of steel wire about ⅛ inch in diameter. It is made a little flat at one end and pointed at the other. With this tool the enamel is carried from the saucer to the piece of work, and it is possible to work the enamel into the smallest cloison by using the pointed end. A piece of clean white blotting paper and a piece of linen cloth are needed to dry the tool on and to absorb some of the moisture from the enamel when it is in place. After the cloisons have been filled, the piece of work is put in some warm place and left until all of the moisture in the enamel is thoroughly evaporated. It is then ready for firing. Small pieces of work may be fired with the blowpipe or bunsen burner, and good results obtained, but the firing is usually done in a kiln made for the purpose.

Champlevé

In Champlevé enamel, cells or channels are cut in the metal to receive the enamel. A partition or border must be left between the cells to keep the enamel from running together when it is fired. When the enamel is applied in this way it has the appearance of inlay. To prepare the metal for the enamel, a cement stick or board is first necessary to hold the work firmly in place during the cutting of the cells or channels which is done with the engraving tools. The charging or applying the enamel is done as in the Cloisonné work. For beginners this method is preferable to Cloisonné as first attempts are more successful.

Painted Enamel

Painted enamel is done on a plate of metal without the cloisons or channels as in Cloisonné or Champlevé work. The plate is shaped or domed a little to strengthen it. In order to counteract the contraction of the enamel on the face of the plate, it is necessary to back it up with counter enamel, that is, to give the back a coat of enamel to be fired at the same time with the first coat on the face of the plate. To make the counter enamel stay in place while working on the face of the plate, a drop or two of gum tragacanth is used. This is thoroughly mixed with the enamel before it is applied and when it is in place the gum makes the enamel stick even when the plate is turned over. When the plate is fired the gum burns out of the enamel. The first coat of enamel on the face may be one of flux, leaving the entire surface transparent, or a coat of opaque white may be used on which the transparent colors are applied later. In painted enamel the colors may be used much the same as in water color where one color is mixed with another to get the required effect. In painted enamel a small sable-hair brush is used to apply the enamel. If, after firing the first time, the colors do not appear as planned, another application is made and fired again and this may be done several times until the desired effects are obtained.

GRISAILLE

In Grisaille enamel the plate is prepared the same way as for painted enamel. A coat of counter enamel is applied at the back and a coat of flux on the face of the plate. After the first firing, the design or decoration is carried out in opaque white. This is applied in such a way as to give a modeled or relief effect. After the opaque white has been fired, a coat of transparent enamel is applied, using any color desired, covering the entire surface of the plate. The decoration being carried out in the white with the covering of color gives a most interesting effect of light and shade.

BASSE-TAILLE

Basse-taille enamels are made by chasing or engraving the design or decoration on the plate in relief. The enamel which should be either transparent or translucent is then applied all over the surface. The different depths of the color on the modeled or engraved surface produces different depths of tone in the color used and gives unusually rich effects.

PLIQUE-À-JOUR

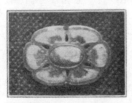

Brooch in
champlevé enamel

Plique-à-jour is something like cloisonné except that it has no back. The cloison or design is carried out or made in the same way as cloisonné. The different units forming the design are soldered with a harder solder than is usually used. When all the units are together it has the appearance of very fine filigree or pierced work. A design for a piece of plique-à-jour enamel could be pierced from a sheet of metal if done by a skillful craftsman, but it requires much care in keeping the metal lines separat-

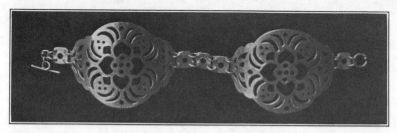

Bracelet ready for plique-à-jour enameling

ing the enamel uniform in thickness and is a much slower process.

When the piece of work is ready, it is placed on a sheet of mica or a plate of fire clay which serves as a background for the enamel. The enamel is then applied as in cloisonné and fired. The enamel will settle considerably when fired but, after cleaning, the depressions are refilled and again fired. It may be necessary to do this several times before the desired results are obtained. After the cloisons have all been filled, the next step is to stone both front and back off, leaving a perfectly smooth surface. A successful piece of plique-à-jour enamel carried out in transparent colors has the effect of a beautiful stained glass window. This process requires a great deal of skill and care to obtain satisfactory results.

NIELLO

Niello produces delicate designs in metal. It is a black alloy composed of two parts silver, one-third copper, one-sixth lead. A brittle amalgam results when excess sulphur is added to this alloy in a molten state and then cooled. Fine powder is produced by pounding and grinding in a mortar with a pestle. Brush a solution of borax as flux into the design lines incised in the metal, sprinkle with the powder. Small articles are fired over a blowpipe, large pieces in a furnace. Repeated applications of the amalgam are necessary till the incisions are filled. When cool, the article is filed or scraped to remove surplus. Water of Ayr stone is used to precede polishing, done with moist pumice and buffer. Overheating the article causes the lead in the amalgam to eat itself into the metal.

FIRING

After the charging has been done, the piece of work is placed in a warm place to dry out the water in the enamel. It is very important that the enamel is entirely free from moisture before firing. The firing is usually done in a kiln made for the purpose although small pieces may be fired over a bunsen burner or with a blowpipe. Assuming that the moisture has evaporated from the enamel and that the piece is ready to fire, it is first noticed that the enamel is now a very fine powder and must be handled very carefully as the slightest jar will displace the enamel and necessitate going all over the work of recharging. The piece of work is placed on a small tray or shovel (page 112, fig. B) made of sheet iron for convenience in handling. A pair of enameling tongs is used to lift the tray or shovel while carrying it to and from the kiln. The work should be held at the opening of the kiln for a minute or two to heat it gradually before inserting into the kiln. After it is in the kiln the enamel should be closely watched as the firing goes on; and when the enamel settles and glazes or looks like a liquid all over, it should be withdrawn at once and allowed to cool very slowly. It should never be placed on any cold substance as it would result in the enamel cracking. If, when cool, it is found that the enamel has settled more than desired, the piece of work is again cleaned as at first, more enamel applied, and again fired. The enamel may be left just as it comes from the kiln or it may be stoned down level with the surface of the metal. The firing process is one that requires a great deal of practice and close attention to get satisfactory results.

STONING

In Cloisonné, Champlevé and Plique-à-jour work it is not easy to apply the enamel without leaving it somewhat uneven when it comes from the kiln. The enamel may be higher than the surface of the metal or it may be lower in places and this unevenness is undesirable. To give the piece a uniform surface it is necessary to work over it with enamel files or stones varying in degrees of fineness. The piece of work to be stoned is held on a pad or board which is placed in a sink or some place where plenty of water can be used. The board should slope away from the worker so that the water, which should be freely used, will run off. The stones or files are dipped in the water and then rubbed over the enamel, back and forth, until the required surface is obtained. Sometimes flour of pumice is used with the stones to hasten the process. A coarse file is used first to rough it down, then one considerably finer and, finally, a scotch stone is used to finish the surface. If transparent enamel is used it is necessary to fire it again just enough to give it a glazed surface. In using opaque enamel this is not necessary. Finally the work is buffed a little to brighten the surface.

Enamel after firing is reduced with coarse files and scotch stones

CHAPTER 14

Modeling and Casting

MODELING MATERIALS

A BOARD, slate, piece of glass or a flat slab of plaster is first needed to work on. The size of this may be governed by the size of the work to be done. For large work modeling clay is used, for medium-sized work plasterline, and for small work hard wax.

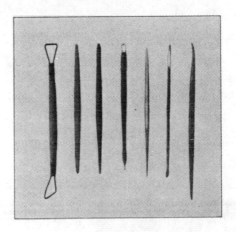

MODELING TOOLS

The tools necessary for modeling, as shown above, are few in number, and should be made by the student, although they may be purchased. The purchased ones, however, always need more or less adjusting and reshaping. Boxwood sticks of various sizes may be had at hardware stores carrying jewelers' supplies and with the use of files and sandpaper they may be shaped as desired. One or two wire tools are found useful and are not difficult to make. A piece

Plaster casts and wax models for various forms of jewelry

of wire of the required size is bent into shape as shown in the illustration and with a very small binding wire is bound to the handle. It is often a convenience to have two different shapes, one at each end of the handle.

Modeling

Acantus leaf scroll

The art of modeling is directly opposed to that of carving. Carving deals with the cutting away of the material while modeling is the art of building up. Although the modeler may be able to add to, take from or change any part at pleasure, building up, not cutting away, is the proper method to attain a simple and direct style of modeling.

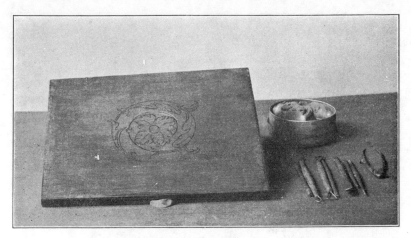

Delineating the form on a modeling board

After collecting the various materials and tools needed, the student is ready to begin. For the first piece select a cast of some good ornament. A white rather than a colored cast is preferable because the lights and shadows are more decided. It is wholly by the strength and shape of the shadows that the modeler is able to see and reproduce forms.

As a knowledge of drawing is absolutely necessary, a certain amount of skill in drawing should be acquired before beginning modeling. This preliminary knowledge of drawing, however, need not be extensive but, as will be seen later, the greater the ability to draw, the better will be the result.

The subject to begin with is a scroll belonging to the Renaissance period. This should first be placed in an advantageous position. Stand it as straight as possible without allowing any chance of its falling forward, and in a position where the light will come from the side and somewhat from the front. In such a position, strong sharp shadows will result.

With a soft pencil, sketch the model upon the board or slate as above. Begin with the stem and be sure to have it the right shape before adding any leaf, as it is easier to see and correct the defect of a curve when there is nothing else to detract the eye from its sweep. If the spiral is not drawn

Starting the scroll with plasteline

correctly in the beginning, it will be almost impossible to correct it when the details are added around it. A piece of ornamental work is a disagreeable thing to look upon if the lines do not turn and join one another in a true and graceful way. Wherever the stem disappears the eye must follow it and find its continuation at the right place and direction. When the stem has been drawn in a satisfactory way, sketch the details, leaves and rosette. This should be done in a broad and sketchy way, blocking them as if they were one big mass. After this has been done, the details may then be brought out. The drawing may be done on paper and transferred to the board by the use of tracing or carbon paper.

The design now being on the board, take some rather thick shellac and give it one coat. This, when dry, makes the plasteline adhere to it more readily.

Now take a lump of the plasteline, roll it between the hands in the shape of a cylinder and then put it on the bench and continue rolling it with the hand, bearing down hard enough so that the diameter is reduced and the length increased in proportion. With a little practice, a long string almost any length and size can be made.

When the string of plasteline is of the right diameter put it on the board as above, having it follow the spiral in the design. Press it down slightly so that it sticks to the board, but be sure to have a good curve. When the stem is all done, start building up the leaves. Take small lumps of plasteline, roll them between the fingers and apply carefully to the board, inside the lines of the design. Do not go over, for if this is done the outline is lost and trouble begins. Keep adding little balls of plasteline until there is a fair imitation of the model. Go slowly and avoid putting too much on. Do not finish one part before starting another but carry the work along so that the same amount of work is put on every part of the modeling.

Remember that no amount of smoothing will make a poor form pleasing to the eye.

In the course of the work, take the model in the hand and look at it from every angle. Holding the modeling in the same position will allow comparison of the curves, and by putting the modeling in the same light as the model and observing the shape and strength of the shadows, it will help to get the profile.

As practice makes perfect, repeat this exercise many times.

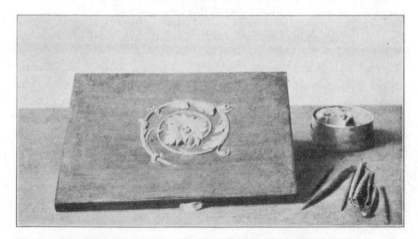

Completed plasteline modeling based on the plaster cast

Casting Materials

Plaster of Paris, a little cotton seed or olive oil and a small piece of soap are all that are necessary.

Casting Tools

A bowl or pan, a spoon, a knife and two or three soft brushes will be all that is needed.

A paper box built around model to confine liquid plaster

Casting

The modeling having been done in soft material is subject to many accidents so that it is advisable to transform it into a material more durable. A cast in plaster of Paris will stand handling without injury.

All tools and materials should be gathered and kept close at hand, for during the casting process there is no time to attend to such things. After the casting is completed the tools used should be thoroughly cleaned and arranged for the next work.

After the final touch has been given to the modeling, the next step, as shown above, is to put a strip of paper around the board to hold the plaster. This strip cut out of heavy wrapping paper should be wide enough to allow one-quarter of an inch as the thickness of the mould and this must be allowed at the highest part of the modeling. Before winding the paper around the board, it should be soaked in water which will prevent it from wrinkling and will also keep the plaster from leaking out. The ends of the paper should overlap about two inches. Sometimes a strip or roll of clay will serve the same purpose as the paper.

Now place a little oil in a saucer and with a soft brush go all over the board and modeling. This should be done very lightly. If plasteline has been used the oil is not necessary.

The plaster should now be mixed. Take the bowl or pan and about as much water as would be needed to fill the space inside of the walls of the paper. Then take some plaster of Paris in the hand and sift it through the fingers, sprinkling it evenly over the surface of the water. The plaster will sink to the bottom of the bowl at first but enough should be added till it is about one-eighth of an inch from the top of the water. Now take the spoon and stir it well, keeping the spoon below the surface of the water to prevent the air from getting into the plaster.

The plaster is now a creamy substance. Take a soft brush, and after dipping it in the plaster, paint all over the modeling, being sure to get into every little corner and crevice. By blowing over the plaster, now and then, it will prevent air bubbles from forming. When the modeling is thoroughly covered with a thin film of plaster take a spoonful of plaster and placing it in one corner it will spread over the modeling. This is repeated until the space is filled (upper illustration, page 130). The board should be tapped on the table, from time to time, while the plaster is being added, which helps it to settle evenly.

When the space has been filled to the top of the paper it is placed to one side and the plaster allowed to set for about one-half hour when it will be ready to take apart.

Assuming that the plaster is hard, now take the knife and place it between the mould and the board (as shown in lower illustration, page 130) and separate the two. There is now in the plaster an exact reverse of the modeling.

Notice that the edges on your modeling have dragged, due to undercuts—which must be fixed in the mould, as it is easy to understand that plaster, being a hard substance,

Pouring plaster of Paris

will not give as the wax did, and should these undercuts be allowed to remain, it would be impossible to separate the cast from the mould. The care taken in fixing these undercuts insures the success of the final casting.

With the small blade of a sharp penknife, go carefully all over the mould, removing these undercuts, changing them into nice smooth draughts so the cast will slip off the mould easily. When this is carefully done, take some soap and a rather large brush (a common painter's brush known as a sash tool, about three-quarters inch in diameter) and

Separating the mould

putting the soap in the bottom of a glass or bowl, pour a little water over it. Rub the brush on the soap till a soapy water results, with which the mould is washed, rubbing it all over and afterwards rinsing the form under the faucet. Now take the oil brush and dip it in the oil and oil the mould all over, then put it to soak in water until air bubbles cease coming out of it.

The mould is now ready. Place a strip of paper around it as in preparing it for the making of the mould, mix the plaster as before and fill to the top of the paper. When filled and before it gets too hard, drive into the plaster at the top a piece of wire bent U-shape, which will serve as a hanger.

Let the plaster get hard, and after trimming up the edges (page 132), separate the cast from the mould by first dipping in water—boiling water is preferable, as it seems to help the separation. If they do not come apart readily, insert the knife between them and they will come apart as shown in lower illustration, page 132.

If care has been taken in fixing the draughts of the mould, the cast will come out perfectly; if not, some parts may have been chipped off, which can be fixed by mixing a little plaster and remodeling the broken parts with it when it begins to get stiff (page 132). As for the air bubbles, if any, force some of the plaster into them and a perfect reproduction of the modeling results.

After trimming the edges and allowing it to dry, it is ready for use.

Trimming edges of the mould for separation

Remodeling the broken parts of the casting

Cuttlebone

Cuttlebone is used in casting special pieces or parts of jewelry when a metal pattern is available. After facing off the soft surface of a piece of cuttlebone with a file, cut it to the required size with the small saw. As cuttlebone is very brittle it must be handled with great care. Place the pattern on the piece of cuttlebone (see below) and press it carefully until it is embedded. Lift off the pattern, and there is a mould which shows every detail of the pattern. If a little fine graphite is powdered over the mould and the pattern again pressed into it, better results are obtained (page 134).

An opening (upper illustration, page 135) into which the metal is poured is made with a small knife. A small vent is made at one side for air. After completing the mould, another piece of cuttlebone is fitted over it and the two are fastened together with binding wire. Moulds may be made in this way for rings (lower illustration, page 135) and good results obtained. When the mould is ready, the metal to be used is

Embedding the model into the cuttlebone

Lifting the model from the mould—graphite powder sprinkled on the mould gives sharper impression

placed in a crucible and melted. A little powdered charcoal is added to cover the metal in order to keep the air from it until it is ready to pour.

If scrap metal and filings are used, a little powdered borax is also added to help it fuse. If the crucible is small, it can be heated with the blowpipe if a melting furnace is not at hand. As it takes considerable time to get the metal ready, it is advisable to have several moulds ready for pouring at the same time. The moulds are placed in a convenient position over a piece of sheet iron or tray to catch metal that is likely to run over. When everything is ready the crucible is lifted with a pair of tongs and the pouring is done.

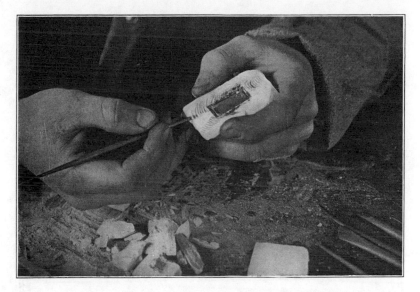

Making an air vent to aid pouring of the hot metal

Separating the mould to produce the casting

CHAPTER 15

Equipment

WORK in jewelry is still being introduced into schools all over the country. It is hoped that the plans for rooms and the equipment outlined and illustrated in this chapter will be of help to those who are about to start work of this nature.

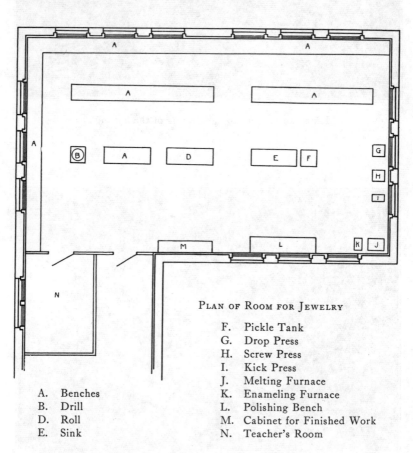

PLAN OF ROOM FOR JEWELRY

A. Benches
B. Drill
D. Roll
E. Sink

F. Pickle Tank
G. Drop Press
H. Screw Press
I. Kick Press
J. Melting Furnace
K. Enameling Furnace
L. Polishing Bench
M. Cabinet for Finished Work
N. Teacher's Room

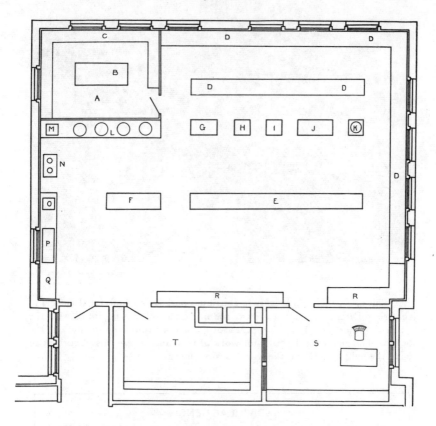

PLAN OF ROOM FOR JEWELRY

This plan shows the arrangement of benches and other equipment for work in Jewelry. The nature of the work requires good light which should come from three sides if possible. The type of bench shown on Page 138 is used in this room.

KEY TO PLAN

A. Coloring Room
B. Sink
C. Cabinet and Shelf
D. Benches for Jewelry
E. General and occasional Work Bench
F. Sawdust Box
G. Roll
H. Screw Press
I. Kick Press
J. Polishing Bench

K. Drill
L. Annealing and soldering pans
M. Enameling Kiln
N. Melting Furnace
O. Pickle Tank
P. Sink
Q. Bench for cleaning
R. Cabinet for finished work
S. Teacher's Room
T. Storage Room

This unit bench and lockers in continuation have six individual lockers so that six different classes can use the room. Each locker is equipped with the outfit shown on page 140. Two pipes for gas and air run along the back of the bench. The method of lighting for work of this kind, where it is important to have the light directly on the work, is also shown.

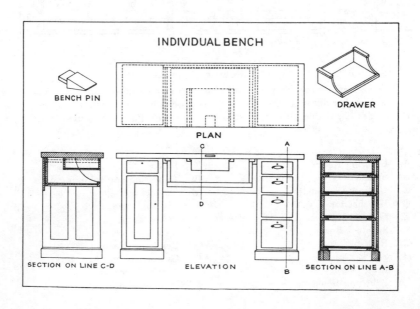

This locker cabinet contains 24 lockers, each is equipped with one pan and the tools shown on pages 140 and 141. For work in jewelry requiring so many small tools it is impossible to keep the equipment together without individual lockers. This locker is large enough for work in jewelry but if the larger forms of metal work are carried on in connection with jewelry more space will be needed.

LOCKER CABINET FOR JEWELRY WORK

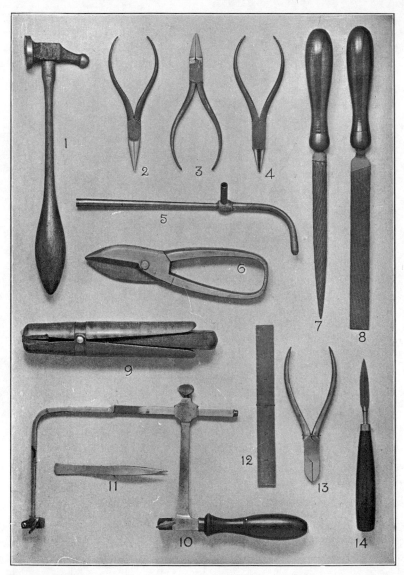

Minimum essential set of tools for jewelry making

AN INDIVIDUAL EQUIPMENT

The pan of tools shown above and the enlarged illustration on page 140 is an individual equipment for school use. The pan is the most convenient way in which to keep tools together; when placed in the drawer under the bench it catches filings and scrap metal which is an important item when working in the precious metals.

The equipment consists of the following tools:

1. Hammer
2. Chain Pliers
3. Flat Nose Pliers
4. Round Nose Pliers
5. Blowpipe
6. Shears
7. Half-round File
8. Flat File
9. Ring Clamp
10. Saw Frame
11. Tweezers
12. Steel Rule
13. Diagonal Cutting Pliers
14. Scraper

Silver bracelets using sheet silver and silver wires

Ring sizes for measuring
size of finger

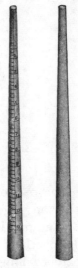

Ring arbors for
gauging and
sizing rings

Surface plate for flattening and
hammering metal

Gauge plate for
measuring sheet metal
and wire

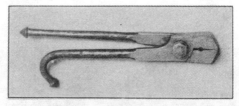

Draw tongs to pull wire for reduction

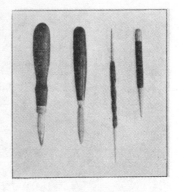

Draw plates may be had with holes of various shapes; the above are square, oblong, and round

Burnisher
Scraper
Scratch Awl
Center Punch

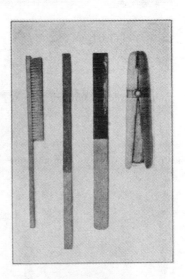

Annealing or Soldering Pan
used for large work

Bench Brush
Polishing Sticks
Ring Clamp

This Polishing Bench is indispensable to any school equipment. As it is portable it is possible to place it anywhere in the room. It is motor driven and has a dust collector and exhaust fan, an essential feature as dust and dirt are unavoidable in polishing.

Roll Top Sawdust Box for drying work after pickling

Flat Roll

No equipment is complete without a flat roll for reducing the thickness of flat stock. With a roll like this one above, and a melting furnace it is possible to melt and pour the metal into ingots and roll it to the required thicknesss.

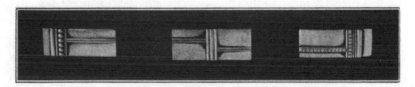

Silver when used with silver wires can stimulate
spontaneous designs in modern trend

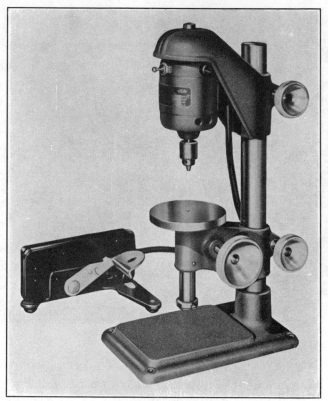

Courtesy of Dumore Company, Racine, Wisconsin

Precision Drill

This Dumore High-Speed Sensitive Drill Press is accurate, speedy and simple to use, capable of drilling holes from No. 80 to ⅛ inch. The speed range is from 2000 to 17,000 R.P.M. with variation controlled by a foot rheostat. The table feed provides very sensitive control for fine drills. The drill and table brackets are adjustable vertically and horizontally to suit work.

Book II

JEWELRY DESIGN

∴

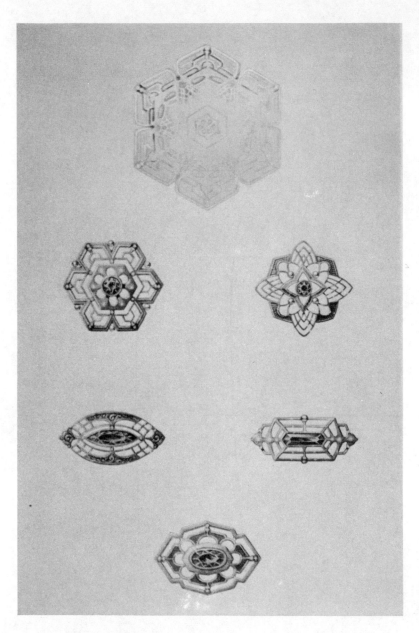

The snowflake applied to brooch designs uses the natural
geometric patterns which emphasize the stone setting

CHAPTER 16

Nature Drawing

DRAWING FROM PLANTS AND FLOWERS

THE boundless field of nature sets before us multitudes of simple forms for study and inspiration. Plant form in all its phases, the world of insects, marine, animal, and bird life, are but a few of the sources for the student to draw from. To the untrained mind they are limited or entirely hidden, but to the student of design with a gift for discernment and accurate observation, they offer no end of possibilities. Learning to see and understand nature comes only after a careful and enthusiastic search for her minute and apparently insignificant productions. The student must first take the flower, leaf, or fruit; the butterfly or beetle; the fish, shell, or the crystal, and make careful systematic drawings, beginning with the whole, studied from all points of view, then passing to the detail.

Studies thus made when translated in terms of design principles, suggesting endless ideas and an unfolding of nature's laws, will be the student's reward.

If fresh flowers are available, make careful pencil drawings of them. The aim is to get acquainted with the floral forms that lend themselves best to jewelry designs, also to gain a knowledge of growth, structure, and color. Cut out a rectangle 5″ x 8″ on a sheet of paper and hold it upright before the spray of flowers. This is called a finder. Move this about in front of the spray till it seems to fill the space in a pleasing manner, avoiding similar or equal distribution of masses. The spray should apparently fill the area without necessarily covering the space. When it has been decided just how the stem is to cut the area it should be recorded by sketching its position on the paper; after this has been done, a more careful drawing is made. In line drawings the shadow side may be accented to give it a suggestion of form or

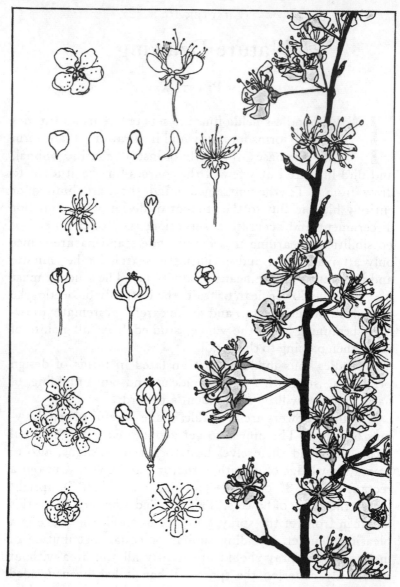

Apple blossom showing natural characteristics and detail

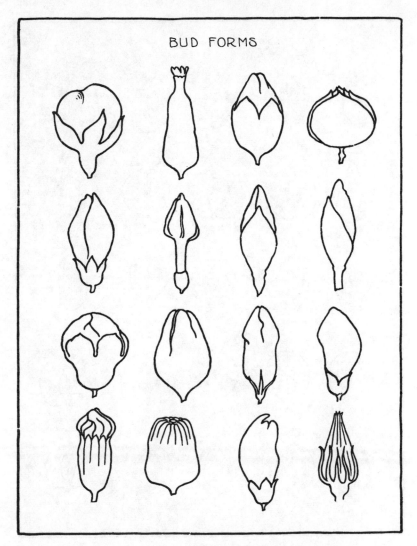

BUD FORMS

Bud forms present beautiful contours when their exquisite
proportions and space relations are recognized

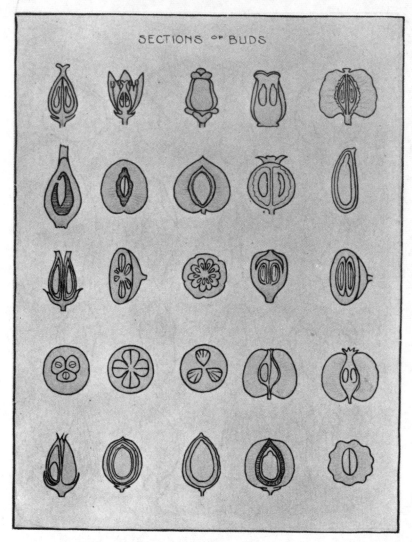

SECTIONS OF BUDS

Longitudinal sections of buds reveal exquisite contours, curves, and proportions. The vertical symmetry informs that nature proceeds by geometry

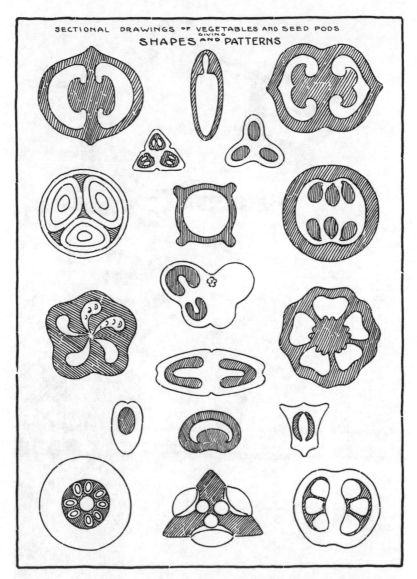

SECTIONAL DRAWINGS OF VEGETABLES AND SEED PODS
GIVING
SHAPES AND PATTERNS

Sections of seed pods make patterns of almost ready-made designs

Details of the peacock reveal many principles of design—
repetition, rhythm, symmetry, balance and sequence

volume. The structure of leaf and stem must be carefully noted; the turn of petals, the swell of calyx, and the spread of stamen, for all this is knowledge that the designer must have at all times. The contour of a single flower bud is quite essential as suggestions of shapes. The color of the spray may be recorded by first inking the pencil drawing (page 150) then filling in with color. Pages 152 and 153 are continuations of this exercise. A thorough knowledge of the different parts of the flowers is highly important in the study of natural forms. The general structure of the petals on the torus, the shape of each petal, the curl of the calyx and the contour of the bud should be studied carefully from different angles, with some suggestion as to their modeling. In this connection, page 154 shows a careful study of interesting parts of the peacock.

DRAWING FROM SHELLS

Sea shells offer much to the student who is endeavoring to understand the beauty of nature. Page 156 shows interesting examples. The spiral is characteristic of many shells and has been used from time immemorial in design. It has rhythmic charm that causes the observer to wonder at nature's exacting work.

Sometimes the spiral motif is quite distinguishable, while at others it bears slight traces of characteristic curves found in other natural forms. The spiral possesses a movement that increases its motion as it seems to wind to the center. It should be recorded with great exactness and precision. Other shells, as the scallop, are characterized by lines radiating from a common point. This shell has been used in every conceivable position and applied in many forms of design. We find it used in metal, wood, clay, iron and paper as decorative ornament. It served in the early centuries as a spoon or receptacle for holding liquids. The rhythm produced by its lines as they radiate right and left from a vertical axis, interrupted with a counter curve concentric

Pencil rendering of sea shells with a mind sensitive to their exquisite symmetry, contours, repetition, details, rhythms, and perfect balances, supply the student of jewelry design with ideas, inexhaustible in stimulation

Insect and marine life, when drawn in light and shade, reveal those exquisite examples of balance, sequence and perfect repetition

with the outline, has furnished many motifs. These are principles of growth that the student is to seek in such nature forms and later make use of in his work. The best way to bring about this result is to make studies that show nature's characteristics exactly as they occur on the shell.

This is illustrated on page 156. The cross-section shell represents lines radiating from a common line. This principle of radiation, from a common point or common line, and the spiral curve, form the acting basis of many designs of a general kind; and of jewelry designs in particular.

DRAWING FROM THE BUTTERFLY

The butterfly, above, with its beautiful spots of brilliant coloring, seems to offer the same material as the shells in the way of order but in a much more charming setting. The main lines of the ribs, radiating into the wings and separating the delicate gradation of colors make an excellent study for symmetry since it is here exemplified in its most perfect form.

The butterfly is rendered with a medium and soft pencil by first making a very careful outline with the medium grade pencil. The shading is produced by laying on the darkest spots first, then the next darkest and so on until the highest lights are reached. Care must be exercised when surrounding lights by darks not to diminish the light areas and to preserve the value for the ribs. For exercises of this kind the

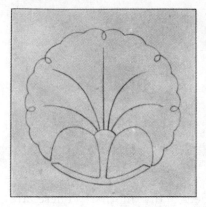

Nature forms in perfect vertical symmetry
sensitively defined with pencil

real butterfly is much more desirable than the colored photograph.

The fish drawing on page 157 is excellent for pencil shading, exhibiting order of lines and masses as they occur in this subject. The scales, fins, etc., offer not only light and shade work for pencil technique but interesting shapes which the student will recall with more importance and usefulness later in the designing process.

JAPANESE CRESTS

Drawing thus far has been for technique primarily and incidentally to see nature from the designer's point of view. Later on the designer uses nature's laws in his own way to emulate its beauty. The illustrations above show fine pencil outline drawings of Japanese crests, illustrating the principles involved in the natural forms previously studied, i.e., lines radiating from a common point.

Pencil rendering from original forms in one even flat tone showing
delicacy of touch and appreciation of patterns in design and in nature

SWORD GUARDS REDUCED

Drawing is now reduced to a smaller scale. The sword
guard, cast, and an escutcheon, shown above, are made
in smaller areas. This requires keen judgment for relative
areas and lines. It calls forth the ability to carry mentally
the measurements from the objects to the drawing in
reduced proportion. The quality of line shown by these
figures is approaching the kind that is necessary for jewelry
technique. The assurance of confidence that is expressed in
every line must be bold and accurate in no less degree than
drawings done on a larger scale.

The exercises chosen for this stage of the work should
possess delicate and extremely fine relations of space areas,
examples that set forth the principles of sequence, balance,
and rhythm in a fine manner. The study of such designs
will inculcate a fine "curve and space sense," if we may call
it such, and will serve its purpose in developing creative
ability.

Ornamental ironwork rendered with sensitive touch and
knowledge of interlacing lines and the involute curve

DRAWING FROM ORNAMENT

The above drawing is a historic example of a fine grill.
This ironwork furnishes excellent opportunity to study the
application of the scroll found in the sea shell and other forms
of natural origin. In historic ornament, as in this Gothic
ironwork, we find these scrolls running on and spreading out
to the double branch volute from which leaf-like forms
emanate; then we find the single scroll terminating in interesting rosettes. The Gothic ironwork of the seventeenth
century on chests, gates, and brackets still survives with its
artistic splendor. It is quite essential to get the spirit with
which the artisan of the iron guild worked. He copied fine
examples with accuracy and precision, thus securing every
little curve and bend of line. Before drawing these, attention
should be directed to the manner in which these scrolls are
distributed over the area, the way the sizes vary and the
small triangular units growing out of the branching scrolls
to fill the space as in the drawing on page 162. After the
drawing has been carefully studied in this way, sketch in,
with single lines, the movement and distribution of the largest
scrolls. The smaller ones are allowed to take their places
and finally the smallest units. This is done in single line,

then a double one is used to indicate the thickness of the metal. Care must be taken not to have corners or flat places on the curves and to represent a gradual increasing movement as they wind in on themselves. Metal lends itself in an unusual way for producing these finely proportioned curves as shown by this drawing. It is hoped that the student will employ these characteristics when making designs for wire work later.

In the example of a Saracenic ornament shown below, we have again the running scroll, only in a mild form. The under and over effect often furnishes many suggestions in design. In drawing a pattern of this kind, one that is divided into six equal sections, it is well to draw the circle with a compass and to divide it geometrically into six parts first. The drawing of the scrolls and units, however, should all be done freehand, first representing the main structural lines of the design with single lines. As in the previous drawing the design should progress from the larger elements to the smaller ones. It will be of help to use as many center lines as possible as these aid in placing the different parts of the design. When these have been located, represent them by a double line. After the design is carefully drawn, shade the dark side with a heavy line and crosshatch the bands that run under for a little distance at the places of contact. This will give it that sense of modeling sufficient to appear woven.

Saracenic design showing over-and-under effect

Door knockers rendered in pencil to gain appreciation
of pattern forms in good proportional relations

The scrapbook is the record and reference source
of the designer

TRACING FROM HISTORIC ORNAMENT

Every student should have a scrapbook in which to keep
such examples as will suggest new ideas or inspire fresh
thoughts. To this book the student may turn in the future to
stimulate the artistic impulse. It is for economy of time and
space that these examples be made on a strong, thin, transparent paper. Tracing from designs to add to the scrapbook
or making tracings during the process of designing should
become a habit. Making good tracings with a clear and
steady line, as those on page 162, is conducive to good
pencil or brush work. The tracing is made by holding the
paper firmly over the model and drawing with a medium
soft, well-pointed pencil. The book or plate being used may
be protected from abuse by placing a sheet of pyraline or
plastic over it. The student should always be collecting
designs, adding them to the scrapbook which serves as a
storehouse of suggestions and is a great asset to the designer.

TO MAKE A SYMMETRICAL TRACING

Very frequently it becomes necessary to transfer a
design from one sheet to another and more frequently it is
necessary to make a perfectly accurate drawing of rough
sketches. To make an accurate drawing of a figure that is
symmetrical on either the vertical or horizontal axis is a
tedious process if the pattern is very intricate, and it is more

so when the design is alike on both axes. Tracing paper will not only save time but it will assure an accurate result. It is quite important to use a good transparent paper and a fine sharp point on the pencil. To make a tracing, take a piece of tracing paper that is a little larger in area than the design. Fold the paper in halves by making a firm crease as on page 165, fig. A. Keeping the paper thus folded, fold again at right angles to first crease as fig. B, making absolutely certain that the first two half creases just coincide before the second crease is made. When the paper is unfolded, there will be two creases at right angles as ab–cd in fig. C, and four quarters, namely 1, 2, 3, 4. Make two diameters on the design to be traced as in fig. D; now place the tracing paper upon it so that the diameters of the tracing paper and those of the drawing will just coincide. While holding it down firmly trace on the first quarter as fig. E. Now fold on ab as fig. F, so that the drawing is on the outside of the tracing paper, then trace the design by drawing on the second quarter of the tracing paper as fig. G. Next fold on the diameter cd as fig. H and trace the half already made upon the third and fourth respectively as fig. I. The drawings of the four quarters, when complete, should be on the same side of the tracing paper. It will be noticed that the design has really been traced three times from the original drawing of the first quarter.

If the work is done accurately with a medium grade pencil, well pointed, the result will be perfect. Now that a perfect drawing is obtained it can be transferred to wherever desired by holding the tracing down, with the graphite lines next to the paper to which the transferring is to be made and marking over the same lines of the drawing. The transferring may also be done by rubbing over the tracing with a coin in one direction only, always away from the worker.

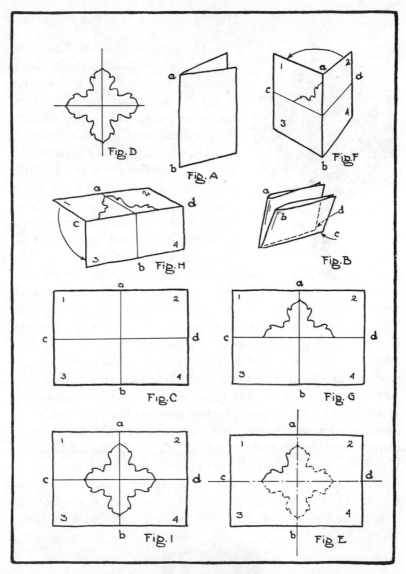

Step by step method of tracing a symmetrical design

DRAWING FROM JEWELRY DESIGN

The foregoing instructions were introduced to acquaint the student with such nature forms as are used in design in general and in jewelry design in particular. The subject chosen illustrated nature's order of growth, the systematic repetition of spots of exquisite color and beautiful curves. Later, historic examples were presented showing how nature's laws were used by man, and the designs attained as a result of following nature as a guide. This line of thought has familiarized us with many ideas of shapes and forms which in turn are capable of suggesting many more. The examples used have not as yet been jewelry designs, but mostly of ironwork, nevertheless paving the way for the smaller and more jewel-like subjects. The illustration represents a fine example of a pendant. It is executed with a soft pencil on paper with a fine texture. The jewelry designs are introduced for the sake of gaining a knowledge of the possible contours and the relation that the stone bears to the general character of the ornament. A knowledge of forms and shapes together with the facility developed with the pencil as a mode of expression serve as an excellent foundation upon which to build. The rendering of this problem is considered under the chapter on rendering with pencil in black and white.

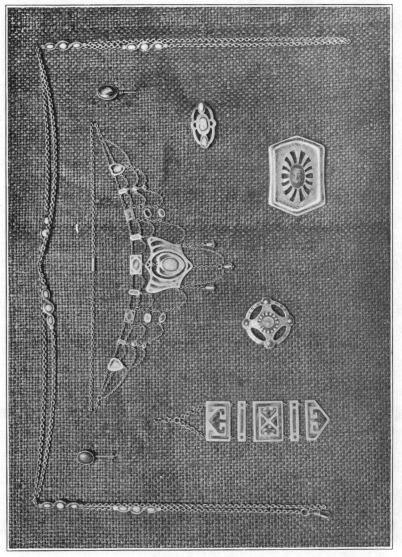

Jewelry display

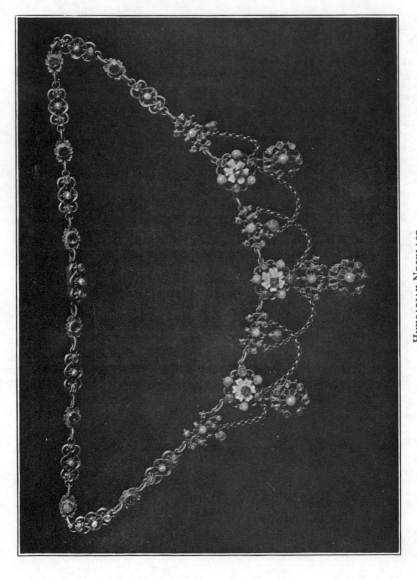

HUNGARIAN NECKLACE

Set with one hundred and twenty stones consisting of pearls, emeralds, rubies and sapphires, and enamel

CHAPTER 17

Principles of Jewelry Design

ALTHOUGH there are many principles of jewelry design, the six that are considered here are first in importance. They are: Fitness to Purpose, Unity between Stone and Ornament, Conformity with Personal Characteristics of the Wearer, Conformity with Costume, Nature and Distribution of Motifs, and Limitations and Possibilities of Metal as a Medium of Expression.

FITNESS TO PURPOSE

Every piece of jewelry must be designed to fit its purpose. Some pieces like the brooch, clasp, buckle, scarf pin, cuff links, and hatpin, may be designated as useful since they serve the purpose of a fastening for clothing. The ring, head ornament, pendant, bracelet, armlet, earring and lavaliere are used merely for personal adornment. As the savage used paint and tattoo to call attention to certain parts of the body, so people of modern times use ornamental jewelry. The ornament on useful jewelry is secondary to its practical value while that on decorative jewelry is of primary importance. Whether the piece of jewelry serves a useful or aesthetic purpose primarily or secondarily, it must fit the purpose for which it is used. It must be of such a nature as to conform to the surrounding conditions, must be duly related to the parts it is to adorn and must serve its purpose in an efficient way.

The ring is circular because it is to fit over the finger. For this reason it must be perfectly smooth on the inside and as it is to come in contact with the other fingers, it must be more or less smooth on the outside. The stone must not rise abruptly or too high above the shank since this would interfere with the freedom of the hand. The shank on the inside of the ring must narrow if the fingers are to close comfortably.

The brooch, which originally was used almost exclusively for holding together parts of the garment, seems to have a place in the ornamental as well as the useful jewelry. It often serves the purpose of a button; for this reason its shape was round, originally, but now the contour has assumed various shapes. Since it is used to hold fabrics it must be free from edges that would catch and tear. It must be made strong enough to hold its shape at all times.

The pendant, necklace, and lavaliere which are worn about the neck and hang over the breast are made up of one or more movable parts suspended on a chain. The pendant is worn over the blouse and must therefore be of a conspicuous size while the lavaliere is a delicate jewel pendant and worn with a low neckline. The gem is usually a small brilliant. It is sometimes used with a chain just long enough to go around the neck and to allow it to hang at the throat.

The Necklace

The necklace is composed of jeweled or enameled units connected by one or more chains; some hang in festoons making a lace-like pattern on the breast. The jeweled units are often graded toward the ends from a pendant hanging in the middle. Necklaces are very frequently set with precious stones and bright enamel. The stones, when graded, produce a rhythmic effect of color. The lace effect is produced by a network of chain giving a rhythmic movement as it recedes from the central feature. In any case, the areas enclosed by the chains should receive careful consideration by the designer. The curves, which apparently begin and terminate on the main line of support, repeat themselves with decreasing or increasing wave-like movements as they lead the eye around.

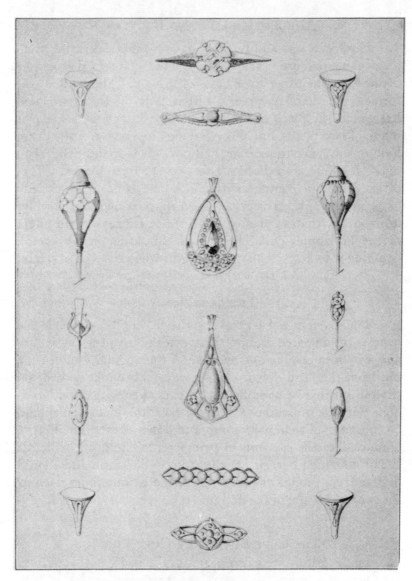

Original designs suggested by the verbena

Girdles, Clasps and Buckles

Girdles, clasps and buckles have a practical rather than an ornamental use. The clasp is made of two pieces, one connecting the other by means of a hook. The buckle was formerly made of one piece, but is now made of two, and has taken the place of the clasp. The buckle as a clasp is made of two pieces, one piece having the hook and the other having the space to receive the hook. It is so designed as to make it difficult to discern the two separate pieces. As it often comes in contact with cloth the contour is usually extremely simple. A very common shape is one that is wider horizontally than vertically. This shape carries out the effect of the horizontal pull. It is made of rather heavy metal, enabling it to keep its shape and form when subject to strain.

The Scarfpin

The scarfpin is used to keep the tie in place. While the head is ornamented and attracts attention to the tie, it also keeps it from coming out because of the angular bend of the pin from the head down. As pressure is brought to bear on the pin it must be of sufficient thickness to withstand bending. Because it assumes a vertical position, its design should be constructed to impart an up and down effect. The hatpin is much like the scarfpin in principle. The head, which is the ornamented part, is usually a knob-like form and should be free from prongs or points. A stone is sometimes used as the central feature of the design.

The Cuff Button or Cuff Link

The cuff button or cuff link is made in various types. It may be a flat disc on the end of a thick curved wire with a bean on the other end, or it may be made of two discs connected with links. It is a necessity, inasmuch as men's shirts are sometimes made without buttons on cuffs. The disc may be circular or elliptical, or even square or rectangular in shape. The outline is invariably simple as it must offer no resistance while being adjusted in place. Ornament employed should be low in relief, enamel sometimes being used. A stone or brilliant is sometimes set low in the metal or, if a large stone is used it is of a low cabochon cut. The wire connecting the two parts is bent in order to bring the cuffs together at the opening.

Unity Between Stone and Ornament

Many gems, beautiful in color and accurately cut, are very frequently ruined by being improperly mounted. The aesthetic value of a stone lies in its color quality. Some stones possess rich and intense colors while others are soft and quiet in appearance. The hardness, transparency or opacity of the stone indicates the manner in which it should be mounted. Stones that are soft and breakable must of necessity be mounted so as to avoid wear.

The cabochon cut stones seem to retain more of the natural qualities than the faceted so perhaps have more charm when used with hand-wrought jewelry. Whether faceted or cabochon, this quality should be carried out in the design. When using stones that are light in color the student should avoid heavy or clumsy motifs. The spots should be rather light, small and delicate in appearance. The ornament, as a whole, should be so treated as to heighten the quality of the stone, making it not only a part of the whole scheme but the dominant feature.

The mounting is a very essential element in jewelry. The stone should not appear to rise abruptly out of the metal but should make its appearance gradually in gracing the whole design. Some stones, like the faceted, need to be set in prongs or in belcher settings since they demand much light to display their color to advantage. Others, like the opaque and soft stones, easily broken, must be protected by setting them low in the metal.

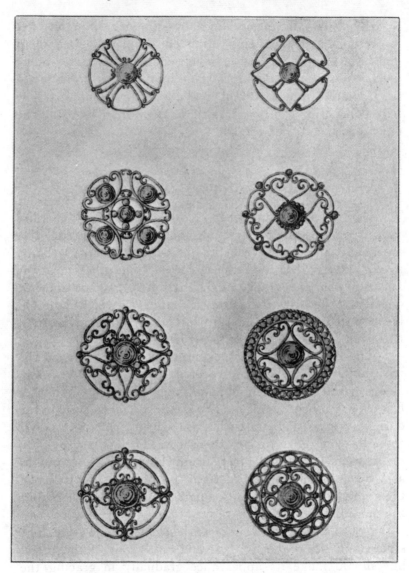

Circular designs in wire based on scrolls of various sizes

CONFORMITY WITH CHARACTERISTICS OF WEARER

Jewelry, like other forms of ornamentation, may be designed for either young or old and may reflect the personal characteristics of the wearer, and even made to express bereavement. Jewelry should be designed to be in keeping with the physical characteristics of the sex. That for gentlemen should be much heavier in design and carried out in a bolder form of ornamentation. The ring is the best example as a contrasting type since it is common to both sexes. The lady's ring is always of a more delicate or dainty character, although the stone may be large in size. The shank is invariably very narrow with little if any design. On the other hand, the gentleman's ring ranges from a medium to a large masculine size with a wide shank having more or less ornament. Men's jewelry today is much less like that of women than in the cavalier's time when both sexes dressed lavishly with luxuriant laces and velvets. Jewelry may be designed to comply with the traits of all ages. For children, it is not only of a small range but severely simple, possessing little if any ornament. Gems of value are rarely used in order that the charm and simplicity of child life may not be disturbed. Brilliant color effects of enamels and stones, richly ornamented with flowers, leaves and scrolls form the bulk of jewelry that appeals to the group that have come into the realm of appreciating the costly material. To this class the finely cut brilliants ornamented with rare and precious metal hold out many attractions. Then there is another kind of jewelry where the design is serious and serene, characterized by soft colors and ornament that is more passive than active. The quality of stones is perhaps less brilliant and sparkling than those used for the younger people. Jewelry is even capable of imparting sorrows and bereavements of life. The design in these cases is often of a straight line character with the customary black enamel.

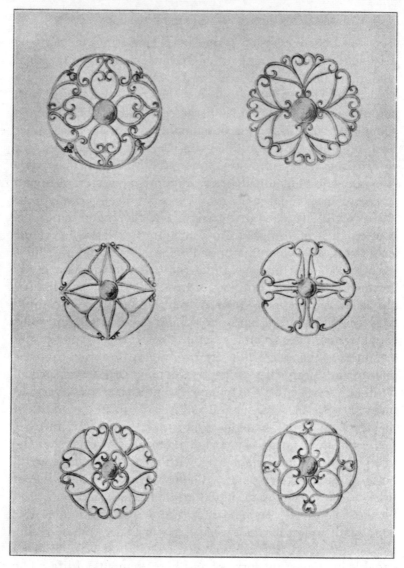

Circular designs showing endless possibilities of the scroll unit

CONFORMITY WITH COSTUME

In order for jewelry to make its appeal it must be attractive enough to challenge other personal ornaments. The design should bear out the characteristic features of the costume. Costumes like those worn on the stage must be seen at a distance, they demand jewelry that will have its effect under the conditions cited. The power of attraction must be secured by the glitter of high polished surfaces and brilliants of various hues, so arranged as to harmonize with the gorgeous costumes. It should form part and parcel of the whole by permitting it to act as the keynote of the entire scheme. The kind of jewelry demanded by the peculiar conditions just mentioned would be very inappropriate for civilian dress. The civilian uses jewelry of normal size, noticeable only at close range. Again the character of the design for this particular jewelry may be made to carry out the style of dress by an ornament that conforms with the costume. If the design is characterized by ornament that suggests action and life it will harmonize with a dress that is perhaps more elaborate. Whatever be the costume, the jewelry should reflect these qualities both in color and in design.

NATURE AND DISTRIBUTION OF MOTIFS

The kind of ornament in a design is more important than even the manner of execution. Some natural forms lend themselves without reserve, especially those that have small forms and that repeat themselves with increasing or decreasing sizes. The leaf pattern with curling stems intersected by clusters of berries has offered many pleasing arrangements. Straight line interpretations delineating shapes of finely related spaces enhanced by fancy wire or granulations have resulted in most dignified and pleasing patterns. Material that seems of little consequence like the tendril with its twist branching out into curl-like lines has been used to develop the most charming and elaborate design. The spiral and the running scroll offers possibilities perhaps as no other motif. Whatever the motif chosen it must be in keeping with the character of the stone, and must be used so as to extoll its beauty. It must be arranged so that the stone is the center of interest. The interest of the motif may lead to the stone gradually, or it may be so arranged as to echo the shape in a concentric or eccentric manner. The motif should bear traces of unity by having a common element permeating the whole design.

Limitations and Possibilities of Metal as a Medium of Expression

Every crude earthy substance or material that is capable of being transformed to a humanly useful object has its limitations and its possibilities. Metal is one of the few substances taken from the earth that is capable of unlimited transformation as is evidenced by various metallic objects in daily use. Gold, silver, and platinum may be rolled out into thin sheets or into the finest wire or made into almost any conceivable shape. These metals can be made into small forms or into granulations of minute sizes. They resist deformation and at the same time yield to the blow of a hammer, which makes them rank supreme among metals. Fortunately, these same metals are capable of receiving enamels to a much better degree than others used more extensively for commercial purposes. However, because these precious metals permit themselves to assume any form it is not in accordance with the principles of the fine arts to abuse this privilege by so treating motifs as to have natural lifelike ornament assume a lifelike appearance. Natural forms chased on the metal must assume a bas-relief effect, thereby retaining the flatness of the plane if they are to achieve their full beauty. Pierced work should not be so delicate as to cause the design to be weak or resemble lace-like patterns.

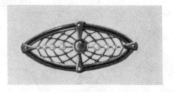

Brooches in gold and enamel

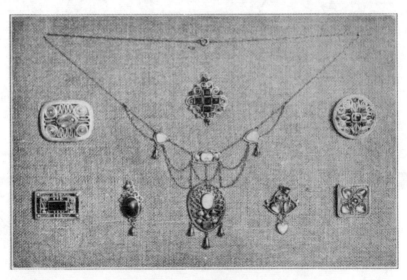

Jewelry display

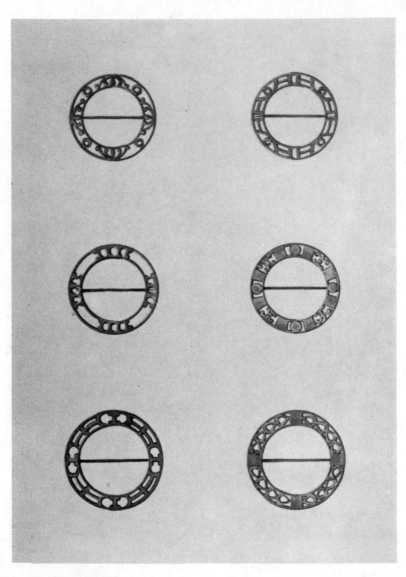

When concentric circles are used as the basic design, the space between the circles lends itself to further design application

CHAPTER 18

The Beginning of Design

VARIATIONS

AFTER the student has made several drawings from various natural forms such as flowers, shells, beetles, or butterflies and from these has passed on to making studies of ironwork and jewelry in order to understand the limitations and possibilities of metal, he is then equipped with experience fundamental for design; but he has not the knowledge necessary to guide him in his endeavor to use natural forms in a design way. Even with a most complete and elaborate storehouse of forms and shapes gained from study, one cannot expect designs to come freely and easily. It is quite evident that there is a gap which must be given due and proper consideration. The gap between studying designs and creating them is wider than is expected. If this gap is not bridged by some means by which the student can easily make his way across from the ability of imitation to that of creation he will find that his efforts will be difficult at the very outset.

There seems to be no better way of bridging this space than by the problem of variation, which lies just between imitation and creation; it takes the work up where copying ends and carries it across to the point where creating begins. Every effort should be made to concentrate the attention on changing the copy even to the extent of sacrificing the technique, in order to obtain a variation of the theme. Making something different from what we already have before us, yet embracing the characteristic features of the model is of paramount importance, irrespective of the practical result. To do this with facility, and in order to record the variants quickly, it is a good plan to do the designing in masses with brush and ink on a large scale before a more careful drawing of the normal size is made with the proper

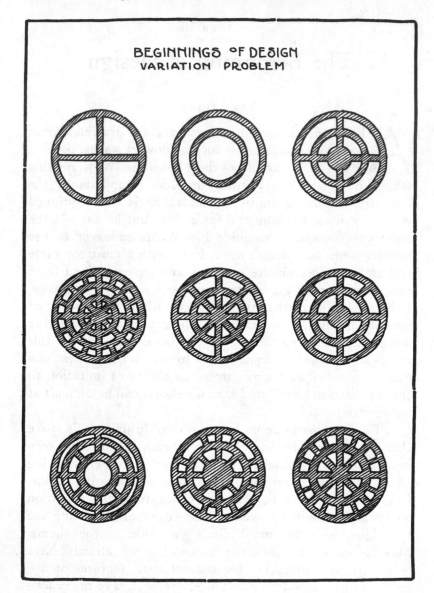

Designs based on circles and axial lines

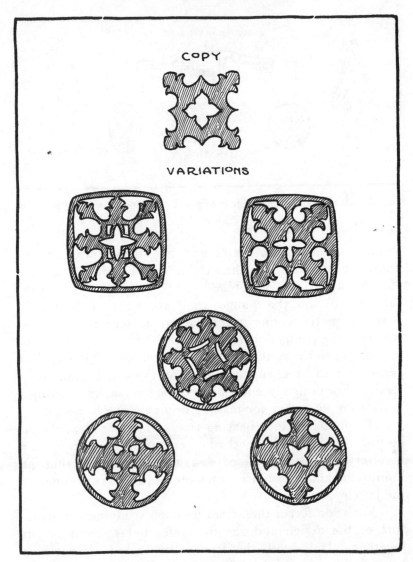

COPY

VARIATIONS

Five variations of a simple design enclosed in circles and rectangles

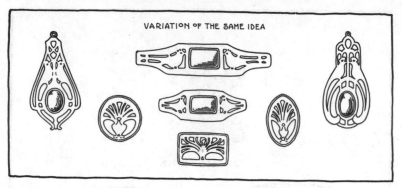

One idea changed and expanded to conform to other contours or requirements

medium. There is no better way to gain a comprehensive knowledge of variations than to imagine a design on a piece of thin rubber being stretched either horizontally or vertically and to note the changes that take place. It is evident that the motif retains its characteristic features notwithstanding the contortion to which the design has been subjected. When the student has grasped the idea that a subject can be varied by changing the proportions or by making a straight line design in curve lines or vice versa, he is laying a foundation necessary for making original jewelry designs.

To obtain an idea bearing traces of the original should be first in mind. The method of executing the variant can be afterward easily obtained so as to be brought within the limitations and possibilities of tools and process peculiar to the jewelry craft.

Variation forces the attention upon studying the structure of the design and the principles by which it is put together. It induces the student to look for something beyond the color of stones or the quality of finish on the metal. All parts are given the more careful scrutiny, all elements are composed to harmonize with each other and with the whole. The relation of motifs, the direction they pursue and the interest they evoke are critically analyzed. The shape of the motif and the pattern it offers is of no little

A Gothic motif adapted to varied shapes

importance. The main structural lines upon which the design is planned must be discovered in searching for the secret of its beauty. When the principles that are responsible for the design are discovered and well understood, they are then interpreted in a new light; this is left to the fancy of the designer. Pages 180–185 in this chapter show several variations of the same theme. This process acquaints the student with the general principles of design and the manner in which others have displayed them. Whatever comparisons are made between the original and the variations they are for the purpose of making certain that the new design has elements common with the old. In adapting the old material in other ways or to new shapes the result may be thoroughly convincing in its resemblance to the original or it may be an entirely new idea.

In working out such problems as those on pages 179 and 181 the copies in metal design should be smaller and smaller till they are the size of the larger pieces of jewelry. Having arrived at this stage we can focus our attention on jewelry and make variations as illustrated on page 184. At the beginning it is a good plan to keep the variation as closely related in character to the original as is possible, as on page 180, that is, not to make a variation that is too foreign to the motif in the design. Later on, when the student's acquaintance is wider in regard to what the ring or brooch or pendant should be, he can easily apply the motif of the original to any form of jewelry as shown in the illustrations on page 185.

The self-contained design at top has been converted into new
shapes and redesigned into new creations

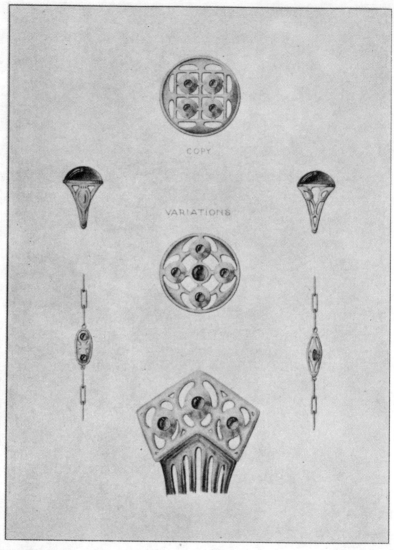

A jewelry design adapted through variation to other units of jewelry

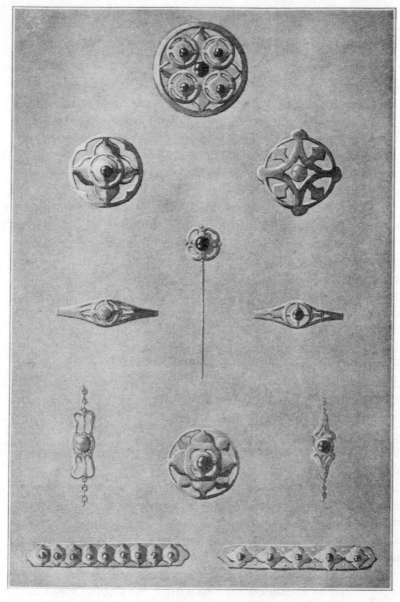

Designing by adapting the motif to other units of jewelry
may be carried on ad infinitum

CHAPTER 19

Structural Elements of the Circle

IF AREAS such as circles, rectangles, squares, ellipses, etc., are systematically modified with lines and masses of an infinite variety, the results produced invariably represent, to more or less degree, either motion or rest. Whatever the character of the pattern, there is certain to appear structural lines which delineate the masses suggesting movement or repose; a static or dynamic quality.

The circle does not evoke any movement if it is small enough to be taken in by the eye at a glance, but if it is so large to cause the eye to follow its circumference then it may set up a feeling of motion. Page 187, fig. A, showing the concentric circles, fails to set up any action, except possibly that of convergence. Fig. C shows lines radiating from the center of the circle; if a concentric circle is described in it as on page 188, fig. R the effect is unchanged. Page 187, figs. N, O which consist of a triangle and a square respectively do not impart any feeling of motion whatever; they produce a static effect. Page 188, fig. S is divided by a curve which suggests a graceful movement. The eye is led through the circle from a point on one side of the circumference to a point on the other side in a rhythmic manner. The added lines in fig. H help to give more motion. Figs. F and G impart an upward motion from a common point. The lines radiate from a center on or near the circumference into the area and eventually back into the circumference with rhythmic motion. Examples of lines radiating from a common point abound in such natural forms as leaves, shells, insects and butterfly wings, and many other nature forms. Fig. H is a variation of the same idea; the lines radiate into the circle from different points on the arc within the circle. Page 188, fig. U is a modification of fig. T. The two diameters have given way to curved lines radiating from the center of the circle, a common point. Still it fails to stimulate any sense

Every design or plan is based on definite structural patterns.
Circular designs when analyzed will reveal one of the above patterns

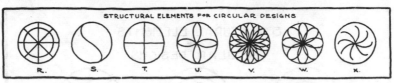

Some circular designs may stimulate totally untraditional
patterns as already revealed by historic patterns

of movement. If these curved lines are multiplied as fig. V
and are allowed to intersect, a movement beginning from the
center of the circle to the circumference and back to the
center is slightly apparent. When these curved lines are intersected by another concentric circle as fig. M, the movement
becomes less conspicuous on account of the added circle
crossing the movement just described. Fig. K suggests a
rotary motion. As more lines are added radiating out from
the center as fig. X, more motion is created. Figures that are
symmetrical on both the vertical and horizontal axis and
have a common center with that of the circle represent little if
any movement, while elements in the circle which do not repeat
the circle and are not symmetrical give the effect of motion.

The drawings in this chapter represent designs in the
abstract; the lines enclosed are structural elements upon
which patterns of the most intricate nature may be constructed. The designs herewith shown have only the fundamental elements; their variations and modifications, however,
may be carried to infinity. Circular designs may be tested
with the structural elements presented here and it will be
found that they will have the fundamental lines in common
with some one of these abstractions.

In creating designs in the circle, the character of the
structural elements to be used should be conspicuously kept
in mind and the result should be consistent with the elements
chosen. In jewelry design, however, such rotary motion as
expressed by figs. X and K, or similar strong effect of movement, should be discouraged.

The ellipse and oval, imparting graceful and varying
movements may be considered variations of the circle, hence
subject to the same treatment as the circle.

CHAPTER 20

The Evolution of Design

PAGE 190 attempts to make clear the evolution of design. The first step in fig. A was the circle and the structural elements. It designated the contour and limited the area of the design. Vertical and horizontal lines were then added. The second step of this same figure has additional diameters. The third step shows a more pleasing result by the modification of the area in the second step made by a concentric band. The succeeding figures, B, C and D, represent the same method of developing designs by the use of different elements. Instead of the circle being intercepted by straight lines we have curved lines within the circle. It can be seen by the different steps how the designs begin with a mere thought in lines arranged in a circle. In each step, either something more is added or some part is modified to make the design practical. Pages 191–192 show geometric construction of circular designs arrived at in the same manner. The figures present elements based on geometry upon which designs may be constructed. The circles are capable of unlimited variation. These plates represent a few ideas which might be varied infinitely. Example, page 192 (lower half) shows the variations of one idea, namely, circles within a circle. Page 193 shows the square with abstract ideas. Whatever the contour used, whether the outlines suggested by these plates or their modifications, all the designs have structural elements. Every design must begin with an idea, either abstract, as those represented by these plates, or concrete, as natural motifs. The success of the design, however, depends on the fine space relation among all its parts. The proper relation that must exist between each part and the whole design cannot be stipulated in words nor reduced to a formula. This can only be acquired by the study of fine examples. The surest way of attaining the desired result is by making many careful observations of good design.

EVOLUTION OF DESIGN

FIRST STEP	SECOND STEP	THIRD STEP

A.

B.

C.

D.

A circle divided with straight and curved lines may develop
simple and intricate designs

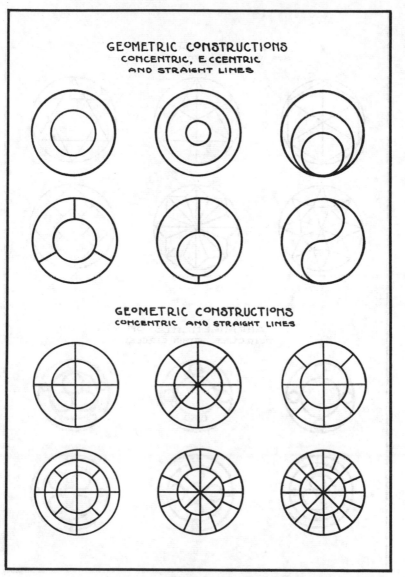

Concentric and eccentric circles and straight lines form
the basis for many circular designs

Circles plus straight lines and circles within circles form
the basis of many interesting designs

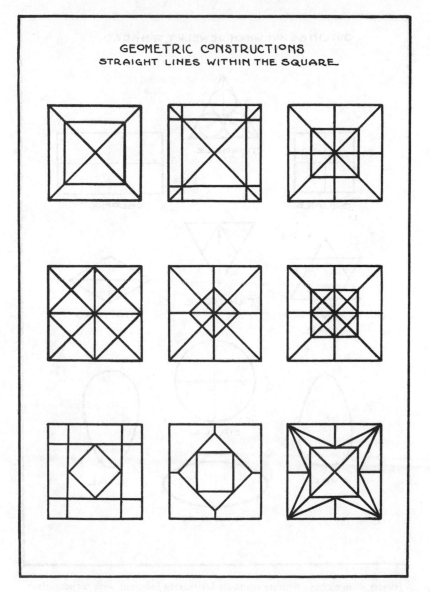

GEOMETRIC CONSTRUCTIONS
STRAIGHT LINES WITHIN THE SQUARE

The square, like all polygons, can be broken up into basic patterns

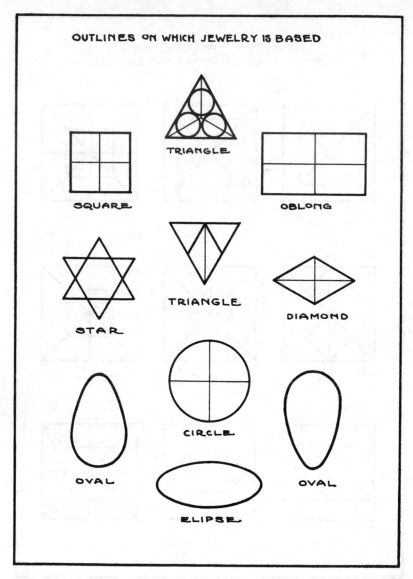

Jewelry designs have definite contours for reasons inherent within themselves

CHAPTER 21

First Problems in Design

DESIGN always begins with certain conditions and restrictions. It is of primary importance that the requirements of the problem are thoroughly understood and adhered to. It should be known what purpose the object is to serve, as this usually confines it to certain limitations and possibilities, and is one of the factors which helps to determine the process of execution. The method of executing the motifs is also governed by the material in which it is to be realized and the tools to be employed. The technical process used to carry out the decoration serves in aiding the structural composition of the design. These are conditions by which the problem is governed and they help toward the solution. The more definite the requirements for the problem, the more it is confined to certain boundaries and ultimately the easier it is to produce a result.

The problem is to design a pierced circular brooch, without a stone, measuring about 1½″ in diameter. The requirements of the problem call for a contour that is circular. The next point to be determined is the kind of motif or ornament to be used and the way in which it is to be carried out. It has already been stated that it is to be pierced. Motifs may be either abstract or characteristic of natural forms. It is intended here to use an abstract motif, and to have the design radially symmetrical. It is to be constructed on the structural lines as represented on page 196, bearing out the abstract figure chosen. The simplest possible design is this figure as selected with plain bands of metal. Modifications of these bands may be made by changing slightly the metal parts either in the perforations or in the metal areas. Variety of spaces, with the proper adjustment of related proportions, adds interest and should be accomplished with a surety of purpose that is strongly convincing. Page 196 represents a circle with the structural

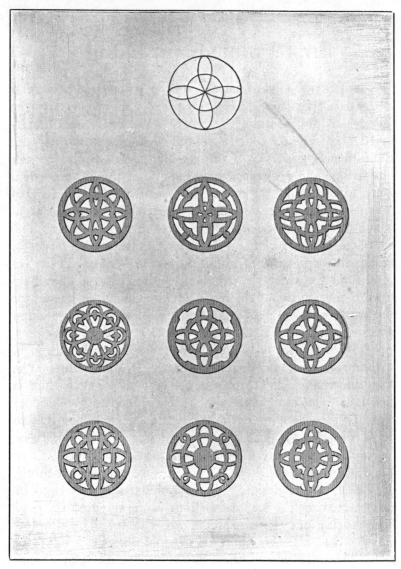

Pencil rendering of perforated designs based on curved lines

lines and nine designs constructed upon these same lines. All of the designs illustrate the idea of curved lines radiating from the center of the circle and intersected by a concentric circle. The designs on page 198 are based on a square within the circle, while those on page 199 are circles within circles and those on page 200 are combinations of circle and straight lines. The designs displayed under each of the pure designs in lines may be rightly considered as variations of the same theme.   In working out these problems, circles $1\frac{1}{2}''$ in diameter should be described with the compass and then diameters at right angles, or radii may be drawn in some of them as a foundation for the structure. A concentric circle may be inserted in such a way as to divide the radii in a fine ratio.

The designer should keep in mind the fact that the lines represent bands of metal. The process should be made free and easy, proceeding from one circle to the other without stopping to make pronounced changes in any one till all the circles have been sketched in. Upon examining the designs it will be found that some are good while others will have to be discarded. The former may be improved by placing a piece of tracing paper over the design and making the necessary changes; in this way we may be able to evolve order out of chaos and at the same time retain the original intact. When a satisfactory number of designs have been accurately drawn on tracing paper, they may be spaced on the proper size sheet and transferred according to the method described on page 165.

After the designs have been neatly drawn they may be shaded in pencil as described in Chapter 21, obtaining a result as shown on page 196.

Whether the brooch is to be circular, elliptical, square, rectangular or any other shape, the problem may be solved exactly as this one of the circles.

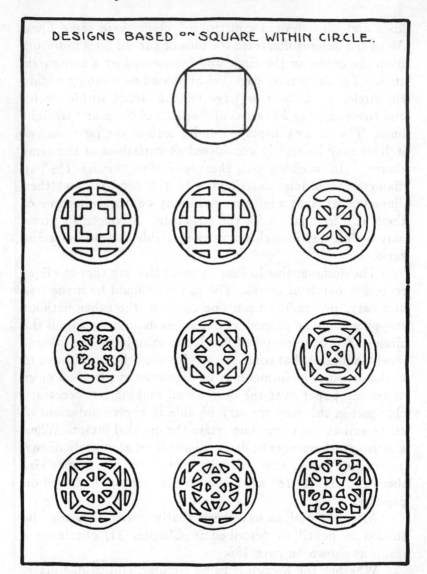

DESIGNS BASED ᴼᴺ SQUARE WITHIN CIRCLE.

A square within a circle dominates these designs

Circles within a circle can make simple or intricate patterns

A circle, a concentric circle, intersected by straight lines
may be carried out ad infinitum as patterns

Chapter 22

Rendering in Pencil

Two Values

IT IS required to represent a flat metallic surface with thickness. Make a copy of a perforated design or take one of the circular designs on page 198. Execute the drawing with a medium grade pencil. The drawing must be accurate and light in its lines. On another sheet of paper practice the exercise of making lines equally distant and of the same grayness, using a medium soft pencil. These lines must be drawn uniform in width, which may be accomplished by turning the pencil slightly with every six or seven strokes, thereby preventing a flat place on the lead, also aiding in keeping a point. The lines may be made about $\frac{1}{64}$ of an inch apart or even less. A uniform value will be the result when even pressure is brought to bear with every stroke of the pencil. Continue this exercise till it is possible to produce areas of even flat tones of different values. Whenever it is necessary to continue the length of lines or to increase the area of a tone, care must be exercised not to overlap the ends of the lines. If the lines are allowed to overlap, a dark streak will appear across the gray tone, which is objectionable to good results. When this exercise is mastered, it will be noticed that these lines, en masse, blend as one smooth shade of gray, producing the effect of a flat value, which is desired. Cover the metal area of the design with these vertical shade lines. When this is done, imagine that the light on the object falls from the upper left-hand corner. This will make the edges dark that are not affected by the ray of light. With a medium-soft pencil draw the dark edges. This gives the flat surfaces their proper thickness. The width of these shadow lines is indicative of the thickness of the metal. When approaching the light they should be made to gradually decrease in width. Page 196 shows designs rendered in this way.

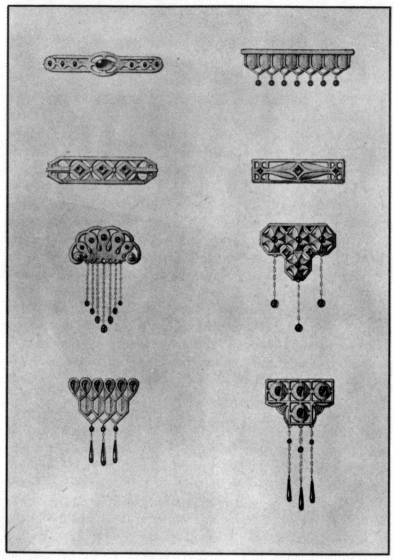

The use of four-tone values gives light and shade in jewelry designing

Three or Four Values

From the previous exercise in line rendering we find that the closer the lines are made the more is the effect of a flat smooth tone. By allowing the lines to touch each other in a lateral position, and with much practice, the student will eventually be able to produce the desired values.

The exercises on page 202 show the lines drawn closer than in the previous ones and the line effect is less conspicuous, which is highly desirable. The examples here shown are not absolutely flat in character but have some rounding surfaces. The high places affected by the light have left the value of the paper while the surfaces less affected have a flat middle gray tone. To render in four values make a number of copies of good jewelry designs. When a careful outline is obtained, represent the thickness of the metal on the shadow side by a heavy dark area. Now introduce a middle gray on the surfaces that do not catch the light as on page 196, keeping the lines close together. Thus far, the metallic part of the object is represented in three distinct values: namely, black, middle gray and white. In some instances, however, it is necessary to introduce a value darker than middle gray to produce more modeling effect. This value is half way between middle gray and black, as page 202.

The cabochon stones and drops are represented with very dark masses of blacks wherever the light affects the stone most. Upon examination of a transparent stone it is noticed that a bright highlight surrounded by a dark appears on the side affected by the light, and that part of the stone away from the light is light, due to the ray permeating the stone. The shape of the highlight must be carefully recorded with the dark mass around it. The dark must blend gradually into the light area of the stone caused by the reflected light and this same dark must make a sharp contrast with the highlight. The different steps involved in rendering a cabochon and a faceted stone are shown on page 216.

MULTIPLE VALUES

Heretofore, the problems have been confined to a definite number of values for the sake of clear understanding and simplicity of representation. The number of values chosen for the previous exercises was such as could easily be distinguished with the naked eye. As the values in the preceding exercises were increased, the difficulty in detecting them was correspondingly increased; e.g., it may be a simple matter to enumerate the planes when a sphere is rendered in three or four flat values but, as the number of values approaches infinity so, the difficulty in counting them increases also. A sphere rendered in many values would result in a fine gradation of values from light to dark or vice versa.

The problem in the next exercise is to render surfaces like that of a sphere; it is a pendant with a large stone, azurite and malachite, surrounded with chased leaves having silver shot soldered between them. Page 206 represents the different steps taken in rendering this pendant although it is not to be understood that the six steps taken to arrive at the finished product is a criterion for all problems in pencil or brush rendering. The approach might have been a more gradual or more abrupt one, but for all practical purposes the six steps seem to suffice for this exercise.

Page 206, fig. A represents the pendant drawn in pencil outline, while fig. B has a dark added in the background of the leaves, thereby segregating them and the same value for the dark on the stone. From practical experience it has been found that whenever shot are soldered to metal parts, as represented by this design, the solder fills in the spaces between the points of contact for a little distance, hence the darks between the shot near the ring and the shot and leaves. In this same step draw the shape of the highlight on the stone and shadow on the ring cast by the slide, as well as the dark on the slide itself. The darks should be a little lighter than desired for the reason that there is chance of making them too dark; if found to be too light they can very

easily be darkened. Fig. C consists merely in delineating the
dark area on the leaves and shot while fig. D has a middle
value over the dark side of the leaves just separated. Add a
light value to the stone on the light area, and to the dark
side of the bezel up to the edge representing the thickness of
the bezel. The drawing, although done in but three values,
begins to look somewhat modeled. The fifth step, fig. E,
represents the addition of a darker value than used in fig. D,
one added to the leaves and bezel but not covering so much
area. The examination of a brightly polished surface like
that of a leaf, with the light coming from the left-hand side
as in this exercise, would show a decided dark just at the
spot where the surface turns away from the light. This
dark is here represented by a value a little lighter than
eventually needed. In this same step the dark of the stone
has been darkened somewhat, also the light part. A middle
value was added to the loop and the ring, taking care to
leave intact the parts affected by the lights. The darks on
the shot have been carefully drawn and filled by a slightly
graded value. As this value approaches the light it is made
a little darker and is made lighter where the metal surfaces
turn away from the light. That is because this surface in
question receives reflected light from the other bright surfaces next to it. Notice that these reflected lights occur on
all of the leaves. A little more dark has been added to the
bezel next to the stone, giving it a convex effect.

In general, fig. E looks flat and lifeless and it is seen at
once that it needs some heavy darks to bring it to a finish. Up
to this time all of the shading is executed with a 2H pencil.
The darks on the stone, as in fig. F, are now darkened with
an HB pencil, keeping darkest those on the right side which
receive less light. Now darken the light on the same side
and let it blend gradually into the light as it approaches the
top of the stone. The left side of the stone should be darkened
somewhat because this area receives less light than the area
around the highlight. If the pattern made by the dark and
light of the stone looks blurred and the edges indistinct,

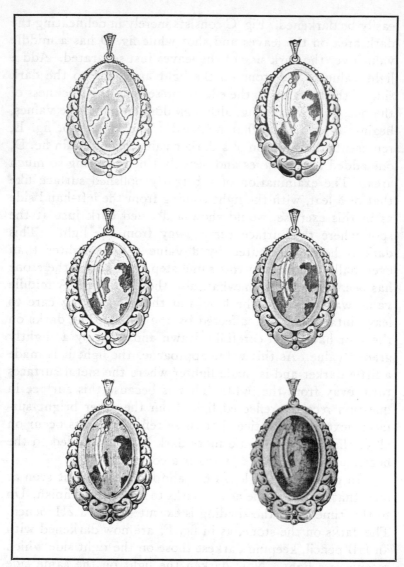

The six progressive steps in the pencil rendering of this
pendant produces a realistic effect

separate them with a dark by using always a very sharp HB pencil. The bezel on the left side next to the stone casts a little shadow, and this made dark will offset the two quite distinctly. Then, too, on the right side the edge of the bezel next to the stone receives the light, hence it is left intact, but appears lighter here because of the dark on the right and left of it. This kind of stone oftentimes has the azurite streaks running through the malachite which is represented by the dark and light effect, hence the fine dark lines, making an interesting pattern. The stone now appears round and real because of the rich dark areas.

With the HB pencil, always very sharp, cover the same background area as was done in step 2. This is done to define the leaves more clearly since the edges next to the darks may have been blurred in working over them. In fig. E one dark was added upon another dark, though covering less area; now over these two darks add a third, covering still less area, and when this has been done on all the leaves and the shot as in fig. F, they should appear to be highly polished. Add some dark accents to the slide and ring. The shadow on the ring cast by the slide should be slightly darker next to the light on the ring. This gradation is due to the fact that the shadow next to the loop receives light from it, hence it lightens the shadows next to it.

CHAPTER 23

Rendering with Brush

IN BLACK AND WHITE

WHEN a discriminating sense for close values has been developed and the fine muscles of the fingers have been so trained that a delicacy of touch results from every pencil mark, the student is prepared to undertake brush rendering.

Make several full-size drawings of sword guards or similar objects on a sheet of white water-color paper. The models chosen should be simple in their outline and pattern as those on page 209. When the drawings are complete, rub them lightly with art gum to reduce the pencil marks to a grayness. Unless this is done, especially when light colored washes are used, the pencil lines will show through the color. With a number 3 brush, mix some charcoal gray and water in a tray, to obtain a value half-way between white and black. More than enough to cover the designs should be mixed. The student should always be generous when mixing paint since it is very difficult to obtain the same value if the wash should run short when applying it to the drawings. With the same brush fairly full of the wash, apply, beginning at the top of the design and working from left to right till covered, leaving the perforations the color of the paper. If a puddle of paint forms at the bottom of the design, first dry the brush on a blotter and then take up the superfluous wash with the dry brush. This should be repeated till the painted surface appears as one flat tone. Best results are obtained if the board is held in a sloping position as this allows the paint to flow down gradually and evenly. When the drawings are covered and the paint is dry, mix charcoal gray with a little water to represent the thickness of the metal. Enough water should be used to reduce the paint to a consistency that can be applied; this value should be almost black. Imagine, then,

Wash rendering in two values reveals perforated designs in a satisfying manner

that the light falls from the upper left-hand corner; wherever the ray of light strikes the edges it will be light and wherever it does not it will be dark. Apply this dark paint, already mixed, for the thickness as illustrated on page 209.

When applying paint in superposition or juxtaposition, the student should make certain that the first color is dry unless a moist background is purposely desired.

This exercise should be repeated till a satisfactory degree of perfection has been attained. The washes should be smooth and flat—free from cloudy effects and hard edges.

The exercise just completed consists of but two values, viz., black and middle gray, as it is impossible to show the highlight because of the white paper used. The effect produced is a flat surface with a dark representing the thickness of the metal.

The next exercise is done on granite rendering paper. The design, which may be original or a copy, should be smaller in area and more intricate in its pattern than the sword guard designs, thereby complicating the exercise. The design is to appear as a domed surface. Page 211 represents the steps taken when rendering in five values. Fig. A shows the design in pencil outline; fig. B the results after applying a gray wash; fig. C same as fig. B with the addition of a darker wash on the right half of the design; fig. D a lighter wash than fig. C with a little Chinese white added. This value covers less area than half of the design. In fig. E the thickness of the metal is represented by the black edges and the highlights by the white edges.

When applying highlights, experience shows that it is better to use the white directly from the tube and apply it with a No. 2 brush slightly moistened. If too much water is used it will be noticed that the white fades into a grayish white as the moisture in the paint evaporates. This means the repeated application of more paint if white highlights are desired. Attention is also directed to the fact that when one wash is placed upon another, covering only part of the area, if the first is dry the second wash will leave a

The five steps in pencil and wash drawings to give a domed
surface appearance to the design

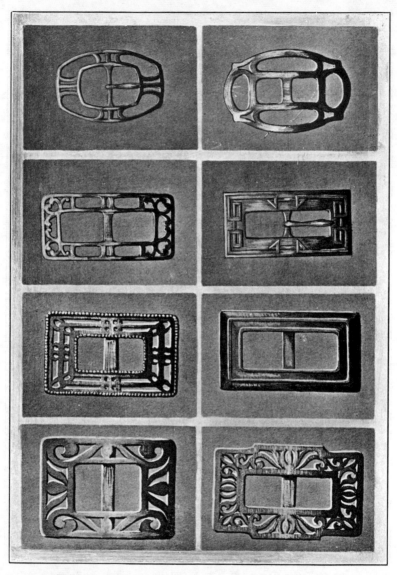

Buckle designs rendered from photographs according to
the method described produce a three dimension quality

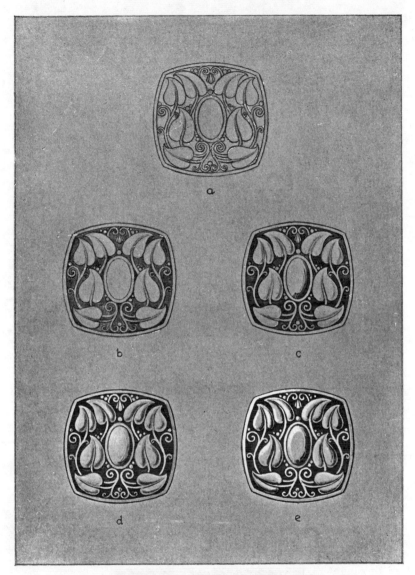

Four-value rendering of original design brings work in relief

hard edge wherever it does not cover the first. This can be avoided if the second is applied while the ground is still moist or, if already dry, by moistening same with brush and a little clear water. To grade one value into another, blend the two gradually by stippling with the brush while the surface is still wet.

The exercise on page 213 differs from the previous ones in that the design is not perforated and has a stone, leaves, and silver shot. The method of procedure is the same as before, kept in four simple values. Fig. A shows the pencil outline drawing; fig. B, one flat gray wash for the background using a No. 2 brush. Fig. C is white mixed with a little water applied to light areas of leaves and stone. A dark has been added to the stone. Fig. D has some dark added to the background and leaves to bring into relief the leaves and stone. Fig. E has highlights added on the lights already added at fig. C, covering less of the light areas.

The rendering of stones in general will be taken up in Chapter 23.

It will be seen in fig. E that the darks for shadows have been accentuated slightly more than those in fig. D. This is due to the fact that the exact value cannot always be ascertained the first time. The study of lights on metals will also reveal the fact that they appear as a sheen when the surface is flat, as represented on the outside rim of fig. E. Throughout rendering, the student should make a careful study of lights and darks and the shapes of shadows, for the shadows give life and reality to the shapes of the lights. Without the shadows on the upper left side of the stone cast by the bezel and the shadow on the light side on the lower right of the bezel, the stone would appear very flat and lifeless.

CHAPTER 24

Rendering Stones

IN jewelry design it is quite necessary that stones be given a naturalistic appearance. To obtain the brilliancy and sparkle with which nature has endowed gem stones is beyond the possibility of pigments. The most that can be accomplished is a reasonable impression of the natural qualities. As a matter of fact, the representation of some gems, such as the very small brilliants, is highly conventionalized. The effect of light on stones, especially the transparent cabochon cut, must be carefully studied. The dark colored ones seem to emit the light so that they appear light on the dark side and dark on the light side with the highlight where the rays have full benefit. The opaque cabochon presents a simple problem of a dark on the shadow side with a light on the opposite side and the highlight at the place where the light has fullest play. The shape of the highlight on a cabochon stone is, of course, curved, due to the shape of the surface. One end of the highlight may suggest the image of the window as a reflection, and the other end may vanish gradually into the dark as it turns away from the light. The stones should be studied and copied carefully till a thorough understanding of their appearance under different lights is certain.

When the student is thoroughly acquainted with different stones, the method of representing them on paper with their respective lights and shadows becomes highly conventional and fascinating. To this end, page 216 serves the purpose of making clear one possible way of rendering faceted and cabochon stones. These are rendered upon a gray sheet, with black and white paints, chosen in preference to the white paper for its advantage in showing highlights. The lateral row on the left shows the pencil drawing of the stones with facets and highlight carefully drawn. Each stone is represented by a top and front view. The light is assumed to

Rendering of stones is simple when the process is reduced to formal method

be falling from the upper left-hand side. The highlights are usually made a little larger in order to be sure not to have them undersize when the rendering is completed. The second row shows the addition of a middle gray, while the third has a dark with lights added. The fourth row is the finished result with the sparkling highlights. The sparkling lights are often applied with paint taken directly from the tube with a slightly moistened brush. The white paint on gray paper often seems to dry out darker than expected after the first application. This makes it necessary to apply the paint several times on the same spot. When using white paper, the highlights may be left the color of the paper, when this is possible. Oftentimes a wash is put over the entire surface of the stone. In this case the stone is modeled as usual and a highlight of pure white paint is used. The same method applies when rendering stones in color.

A quicker method of rendering cabochon stones, especially the opaque kind, is to first lay on a flat wash of color, then with a little graphite on the point of a shading stub darken the shadow side, making it grade into the light area gradually. While this subdues the intensity of color somewhat, the effect is nevertheless satisfactory. The highlight is then applied in the usual way. A careful study of the dark area of a stone, front and top views respectively, will determine the shape of the dark and the customary place for the highlight. When the stone is represented in a box setting, it will have the advantage of the metal around it, with its light and dark effect, to offset the gem. The little shadow cast by the thickness of the bezel on the light side of the stone and the light of the bezel on the dark side also help to separate the stone from the surrounding ornament.

As it is impossible to represent all the facets on very small diamonds, it is necessary to reduce the number of the facets to as few as will adequately explain the gem. Stones not larger than one-eighth inch fall in this class. A circle is first drawn with a fairly hard pencil, then two equilateral triangles are inscribed, freehand, one with its apex in line with an imaginary vertical diameter, and the other with a vertex diametrically opposite the apex of the first triangle, making a six-pointed star. A very light blue wash is then placed on the entire stone and, when dry, a darker blue is placed on the central area, the table, the hexagon enclosed by the lines of the triangle. The lines on the light side are then represented by white lines, while those on the dark side are kept in their relative values. A highlight drawn parallel to the direction of the falling ray is also placed on the table and on the portion away from the falling light. A little dark of the same value as was placed on the table is added in the angles made by the lines of the triangle. The dark is added only in a few places especially on the light half of the stone and in those angles away from the direction of the falling rays. A touch of pure white is applied on the intersection of the lines forming the triangles. This should be repeated till the lights appear to sparkle.

This pendant combines rhythmically the curve of grace with a simple natural leaf

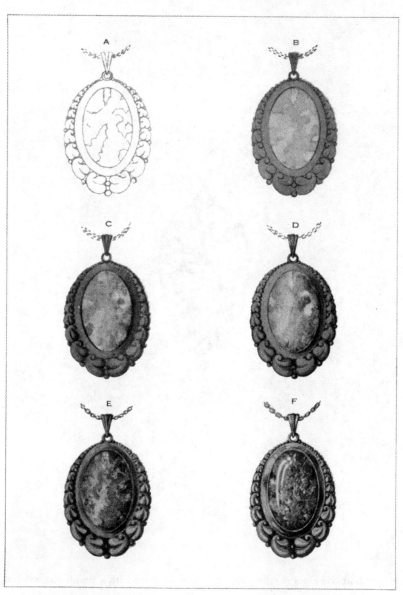

Six steps in color rendering of original design for gold pendant

Chapter 25

Rendering in Color

IN method, this exercise is the same as Chapter 22 except that the problem is much more intricate since it has more than four simple values. Instead of using black, white, and various tones of grays, we use yellows, red-oranges and browns representing gold colors. The colors here used are pale cadmium or gamboge, Van Dyke brown, vermillion, Chinese white and black. Since there are many shades of gold, no attempt is made to give a recipe for any one special shade. Cobalt blue and various shades of green graded with its complement or black was used for the stone.

Plate (left), fig. A, shows the pencil drawing slightly rubbed with art gum to gray the blackness of the pencil marks; fig. B shows the metal part of the design covered by a flat gamboge yellow wash, using a No. 2 brush. The stone is washed in with pale blues and greens. Fig. C shows the addition of one dark on the shadow side of the motifs in relief, and shadows cast by the bezel on the stone. For this part of the work a No. 1 brush may be easier to handle although this depends largely on individual ability. Fig. D shows that some darker values have been added in places. The dark is the same as that in fig. C with a little more Van Dyke brown. It should be noticed, however, that as the darks are darkened they lose life and metallic quality unless a touch of Alizarian crimson is added. Fig. D shows the stone worked up more by darkening the blues and greens and the form of the stone modelled. Fig. E shows the lights applied, viz., pale cadmium mixed with white for that part of the metal that catches the most light. The darks have been accentuated in places and the colors of the stone darkened on the dark side. Fig. F shows the added finishing touches. A careful study of a highly polished piece of jewelry with relief work will have some reflected lights due to the adjoining surfaces. These lights are represented in the drawing with pale cadmium and a touch of red-orange. The last is added to give the color more warmth since these reflected lights are not exposed to much light. The last design, F, seems full of light and life. The metal appears to have a bright polish and the high places sparkle with much brilliancy. This is obtained by adding a little more white to the yellow used for the lights in fig. E. These light yellows, when applied, should cover less area than those in fig. E. When all the lights have been gone over by this last yellow, viz., pale cadmium and white, the highlights are then ready to be applied. These highlights, which are used sparingly, are made by applying pure white paint from the tube with the No. 1 brush slightly moistened. The highlight on the stone is pure white paint.

An ensemble of jewelry emphasizing one motif

CHAPTER 26

The Vital Curves

CURVED lines may be graceful, weak, or forceful, and varying or monotonous. Curves abound in nature from the humble plant to its most charming creations. We must select the lines which are most pleasing and fascinating to the eye in creating designs.

Human nature delights in variety and is intensely interested in change, especially when it occurs at varying intervals. Variety of action, work, and scenery often give buoyancy and spice to life. Human nature often craves for change; but if it occurs too frequently, we have a condition of unrest which is even more undesirable than monotony. The question arises as to how much change we can stand without reaching the point of abusing variety to such an extent that we cease to appreciate its value. This depends upon the physical and psychological conditions and upon individual differences. While the interest in a mere line does not depend on all three of the above conditions, it does rely on the aesthetic turn of mind and on temperament.

A line reaches its supreme beauty when it changes gradually with a slight increasing or decreasing variety for a certain length of its course and then makes a sudden and quick turn to the end. Such a curve is free, stimulating and graceful; it leads the eye slowly but surely for a considerable distance along a flat curve when it hastens the eye to the end with increasing and varying momentum. The changes in such a line often occur in a geometrical progression.

THE CURVE OF GRACE

The curve of grace, fig. A, page 225, may be made mechanically, by striking a series of arcs with different centers, but it can best be produced freehand with the sense of feeling as the only guide. Fig. A which typifies this curve was drawn as just explained. Nature has imprinted this curve on many forms; the nautilus shell is a striking example of wonderful grace. A careful study of the shell shows how this curve quickens its movement with increasing momentum as it winds toward the center. Here again we have exemplified an arithmetical progression of varying intervals of motion that pleases the aesthetic sense. Its graceful movement has been recognized as one possessing a supreme quality of beauty, hence its use in various applications. The Egyptians used it on their painted borders, the Greeks made extensive use of it in their decorations as a running border, the Romans employed it in their Ionic capitals and it was appreciated to such an extent as to find a happy combination with the Corinthian capital of the composite style. The Gothic craftsman of the 16th and 17th century found its ready application in iron and the precious metals. The iron grills, the large church door hinges, consoles in architecture and the metal attachments on wooden chests are but a few examples where the spiral found expression. In all the fine examples that have survived we find the spiral was executed with the utmost skill and perfection. The delicate acceleration of motion in each spiral is brought to the highest perfection in feeling and execution. The illustration on page 226 is as fine an example of a double branched volute curve in its application as can possibly be found anywhere; the acme of beauty. The curve of this ironwork should be studied and copied many times, nay, worked out in the metal before it can be appreciated. The goldsmith and jeweler of the guild made use of it in more ways than one. We find the scroll of many more turns in delicate filigree work. This is made possible by the softness of the gold or silver wire used. Oftentimes these spirals, making a double branched volute, are used in a series to make current scrolls.

THE CURVE OF FORCE

The curve of force, fig. B, page 225, occurs profusely in nature as a supporting element. Its seemingly straight part implies strength, it gives the feeling of being able to give great support. It is found in many plants, ranging from the blade of grass to the contour of the tall elms. It is the beautiful curve that the skyrocket describes as it leaves the ground in an almost vertical direction, increasing its curve to the top as it loses momentum, until from lack of force it quickly takes a downward direction producing the same curve once again in the reverse. The eye delights to follow it as it ascends high into the sky, not only because of the path it describes, but also because of the varying speed it generates. This curve is also to be found in the oval and the ellipse, but is absent in the circle. It will readily be seen that the circle lacks variety because, by reason of its sameness of curvature, any part of its circumference can be superimposed on any other part, hence its monotony of curvature. It continually changes direction; at every point on the circumference the change is unvarying since it eventually returns into itself. The curve of the circle is not a free curve as it is controlled by a center. It is seldom found in nature except in the cross section of stems, stalks, and tree trunks. Ruskin calls it the finite curve, while the free curve of the oval and the ellipse he designates as the infinite and immortal curve of beauty.

We find the curve of force used by the people of past generations; the Egyptians recognized it in the lotus bud, and papyrus, they found a direct application in their capitols; the Greeks showed their fondness for it as is evidenced by the contour of their vases, the antifix, akroter and in many other sculptural ornamentations. It did not escape the keen eye of the Romans, as we find it used profusely on their painted vases, their capitals, arches, and even their small common bronze utensils. The curve of force is capable of so much variation and offers endless possibilities. The ingenious designer can easily imagine the reverse curve of this line and make it readily applicable to many forms and contours. Such a line makes an "S" curve and by changing its proportions it can assume infinite variety as is shown on page 225, fig. C, it may assume such a perfection as to make what Nogarth regards as a curve of beauty.

THE CURVE OF BEAUTY

We have observed this line in the rolling hills of the country as they merge one into the other; we recall it in the upward sweep of active flames and in the rolling waves of the high seas. We find it throughout the contours of the human figure when in profile. The artist in recognizing this line of beautiful movement and fine proportion has not failed to use it in his own expression of thoughts and emotions. Master Painters like Giotto, Michaelangelo, and Titian, not only made frequent use of it as the main structural lines of their theme but the composition of a single figure or drapery was made to echo the movement. Corot made frequent use of it in a horizontal position. His points of attraction and general massing of darks cause the eye to move unconsciously in the path of such a curve. The grandeur of his whole composition is largely due to his success in making the elements conform to this exquisite line of beauty. The sensation and joy stimulated by the subtle movement of such curves can be likened to the rhythms of a great symphony.

It is the province of jewelry design to use anything that is grand and ennobling. Employing the most precious metals, bits of exquisite colored enamels, gems and pearls of the rarest specimen, it only seems compatible with the above to make use of the line of beauty as a means of unifying metal and stones. Thus the artisan may express his inner feelings and emotions in the mediums just mentioned as the artist does with paints, brushes and canvas. The jewelry craftsman, however, cannot use curves of an intricate kind if he would observe the use to which his product is to be put. It limits him to simple and restrained lines with a variety of the most subtle kind. Hence his sensitiveness to so fine a curve as herewith described.

The designs on page 225 show the application of these three fine curves in brooches and lavalieres. They have been

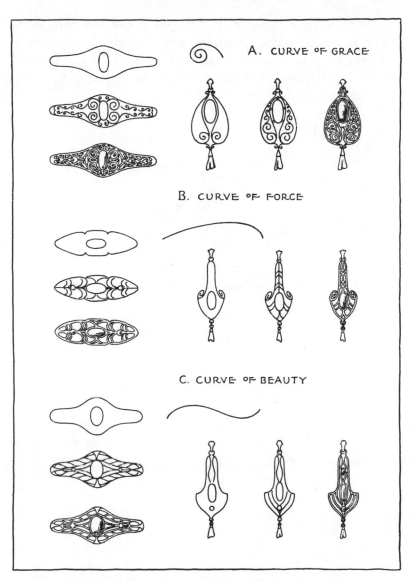

A. CURVE OF GRACE

B. CURVE OF FORCE

C. CURVE OF BEAUTY

The use of these three curves give simple designs of good
line arrangements and fine relationships

made to assume apparently different curves by combining them in unique ways. In some cases, the same is repeated in varying sizes, in others the same curve is placed end for end, while in still others they have been so combined as to create the movement of running scrolls.

An example of superlative scroll
design, comparable in fineness
to the Greek Parthenon

CHAPTER 27

How to Choose Material for Jewelry Design

IN the foregoing chapters, evidence was given of such natural forms as the shell, beetle, butterfly, flower, feather, etc., as material which is full of decorative motifs, and particularly because they lend themselves to jewelry design very easily.

The sources of design from which may be obtained suggestions for new ideas are countless to the student whose mind has been so cultivated as to see ideas in whole or in the parts of things. It is needless to say that all things in nature are not suitable for this particular branch of design, hence the student must be discerning in his choice of material. From the material which we have selected we can easily see by a rough analysis that it has certain principles of order in common. We find in most of these a certain repetition of shape, a rhythm of line and shape, symmetry on a vertical or horizontal axis, and the principle of order of some kind.

Yet we may look around us and find much in the world of animal or plant which contains these principles and yet is not quite suitable for our particular line of design, simply because it does not lend-itself easily to the character of the jewel. The material chosen should be made up of small units which, if repeated in groups, will form a beautiful pattern, and if taken separately will give fine shapes. This can easily be seen in such material as has been mentioned above, also very strikingly in the seed pod or in a bud of a flower when a section is taken. The material chosen should be full of motifs which are beautiful in themselves and which, if placed side by side and repeated in a circle or a square, will make a fine pattern or a beautiful spotting.

CHAPTER 28

Designs Derived from Nature

"Though we travel the world over to find the beautiful, we must have it with us or we find it not." —EMERSON

IN designing jewelry we may use abstract elements which of themselves have no definite meaning nor suggest any natural form, or we may go to nature and use plant, bird, marine, and insect life, for suggestive motifs. However well the student may know and be able to represent natural forms, he cannot use them as designs in any material unless he adapts them. Adaptation is the keynote to applied design. When the motif is adapted, it forms an integral part of the material employed, and the transition through which it passes is called conventionalization. This does not mean that the subject matter is put through a formalizing or stiffening process whereby beauty and life become extinct, but that it is interpreted in a decorative manner, emulating nature's beauty, growth, and color in the material employed, creating, as it were, a new form.

Nature's source of wealth for motifs is vast and unlimited but the student cannot use them unless he has learned wherein the beauty lies, through the study of such forms. The flower or other subject matter should be studied carefully, line for line, turning it first one way and then another, and recording the most interesting aspects. The relation of lines and masses should be looked for and recorded as it appears to proclaim the most characteristic aspect. Perhaps the grouping of the petals about a common center or the relation of stamen and swell of calyx exemplifies its beauty. The contour of the leaves and drooping of the flowers may make a strong aesthetic appeal. The beauty may not be evident at the first inspection but may reveal its charm only as the flower is viewed with careful scrutiny and understanding from different angles.

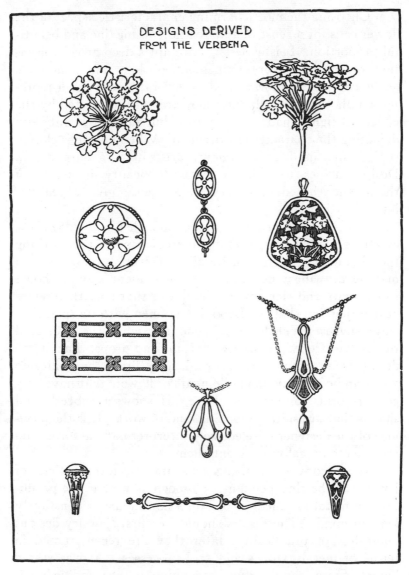

DESIGNS DERIVED
FROM THE VERBENA

Nine applications to jewelry design derived from the verbena

Choosing the most charming characteristic aspect of the flower calls for a sense of appreciation of fine line and beautiful proportion. It is useless to attempt a decorative translation of nature before refinement of line and space are achieved. Natural forms used as decoration are never represented photographically, i.e., they are not interpreted by the effects of light, shade, and texture, but rather decoratively, depicting the character as ornament. When nature is closely copied and used as ornament, art suffers a sure death. Design strives to enhance nature's beauty in terms of the medium used and does in no sense give a realistic interpretation.

The illustrations, pages 229, 232, 234 and 235, show careful drawings of sprays in different aspects representing the characteristic growth, detail of flower, leaves, etc. In making drawings such as these the student should choose those views and elements of the flower that lend themselves best to jewelry shapes. Drooping stamen with its spreading calyx suggests such forms as pendants, while the buds lend themselves freely for scarf or hatpins and drops. Facility to design from nature will depend largely upon the ability to select and conventionalize elements of flowers that have suggestive forms for jewelry. Page 231 shows the beetle and shapes that are suitable for this kind of work. It is the province of the designer to selectively interpret natural forms and not microscopically represent them.

When conventionalizing a naturalistic form, articles of jewelry as the ring, pendant, or brooch as well as the peculiarity of metal as a medium of expression should be constantly kept in mind. The results should be: first, jewelry designs regardless of practicality; later they are reconstructed in terms of metals, stones and tool processes. As was stated before, there is no virtue in copying nature and using it bodily for decorative purposes. If it is desired, however, to maintain the characteristic features of some particular flower so that its identity is obvious, the natural growth of flowers, petals, and detail used should be conventionalized

Nature furnishes many interesting and novel contours

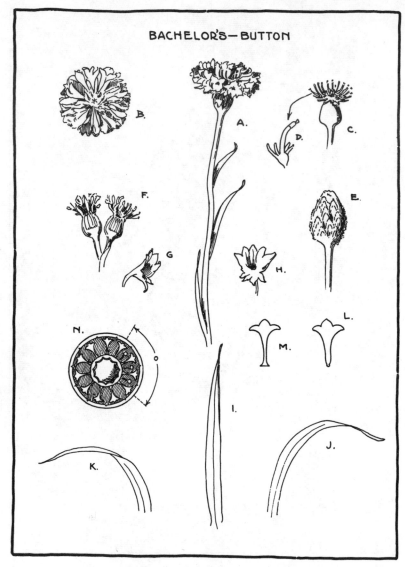

The enlargement of parts of bachelor's-button suggests
conventional designs for jewelry

consistently throughout the pattern. Design demands uniformity of change throughout the process. If the plant form is used only as a suggestive motif, the amount of departure from the naturalistic is arbitrary. It may be so highly conventionalized as to entirely lose the identity of the source, as some of the designs on page 234. The proportions of the elements may be changed to suit the idea the designer has in mind, e.g., if the unit is long and narrow and suggestive of a bar pin, it may be made short and wide through the middle or at one end for a brooch or pendant. It is quite evident in conventionalizing that it is not necessary to keep the proportion of the naturalistic form and that it may be modified to suit the needs of the problem at hand provided it is done in a fine way. On page 245 the manner of growth and contour of the leaves and smaller units with bell-shaped flowers have been arranged to suit the outline of the pendants and brooches. These same designs in turn may serve as suggestive ideas for future designs. The illustration, page 232, fig. A, is a bachelor's-button. The flower was studied carefully from different angles, observing growth, contour, lines, masses and color of leaves and flowers. The most interesting aspects were drawn as figs. A, B, C, etc. Details showing enlargement of different elements were carefully recorded, as D, G, H. For extended study, the petals were turned down and the flower opened. Drawings were then made as it appeared from the front and top. Buds were dissected transversely and longitudinally, as shown by fig. F. The knowledge derived in making these drawings is invaluable when making conventionalized designs of them; fig. L is formal interpretation of G and H.

Thus far the drawings are mere records of this particular flower, although there is some slight modification in the proportion of the elements. In order to serve the purpose of decoration they must be subjected to more change. They are now ready for adaptation or conventionalization.

In adapting designs to metal, the student must ever keep in mind the processes that are involved in making jewelry.

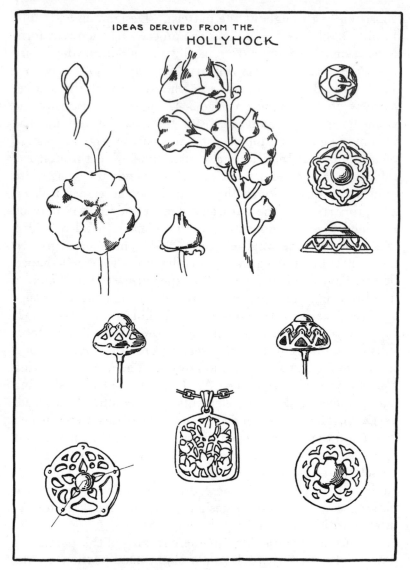

IDEAS DERIVED FROM THE
HOLLYHOCK

The hollyhock seen through the eyes of a designer can yield
many interesting designs for jewelry

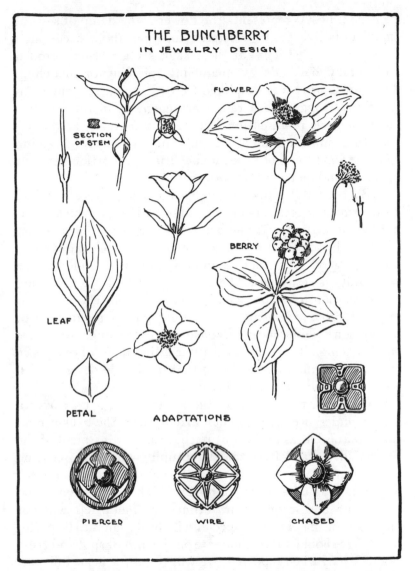

THE BUNCHBERRY
IN JEWELRY DESIGN

FLOWER

SECTION
OF STEM

BERRY

LEAF

PETAL   ADAPTATIONS

PIERCED   WIRE   CHASED

Simple flowers when seen in terms of design principles
stimulate many practical ideas

Page 232, fig. A, represents the flower as made up of several small units like fig. G, clustered together about a common center as in B. This at once suggests a circular brooch which may be made by enameling, piercing or modeling. The unit G or H was simplified as M, L, the arrangement in the flower suggesting a radial arrangement in the jewelry. Hence a circle representing a stone as a center of attraction with these units around it at regular intervals as N. In doing this, the aim should be to secure beautiful proportion between openings and metal.

By beautiful proportion is meant a fine space relation. Two or more spaces may be in good or bad proportion according to the relation that one bears to the other. The contrast must not be too great nor must they be too much the same in area. In good proportion, monotony is absent while variety with unity is desirable. There is no definite ratio regarding space relation to denote when spaces are well related. Feeling and good judgment are the only guides to fineness of proportion. Differences of space are not enough to assure good spacing. There must be a fine adjustment of one space with another in order to obtain that quality in design which gives everlasting joy and pleasure.

However, there is no virtue in repeating a unit over a surface unless we give as much attention to the background space that is left as to the unit itself. A fine adjustment of the units and metal left is the determining factor in securing good proportion. One spot should help the other and the whole should be free from confusion. If the unit chosen is too broken up and irregular in outline, the metal left will not make a pleasing pattern, especially if the design is to be perforated. We should not concentrate on the unit or spot and trust to luck that, when repeated, we will obtain a beautiful pattern in the background metal left after piercing. The pattern made by the motifs and the metal after the motifs are modified according to the process chosen should be thought of as one.

It will be seen that on page 232 fig. N has been modified in its repetition and a unit added. The unit was improved

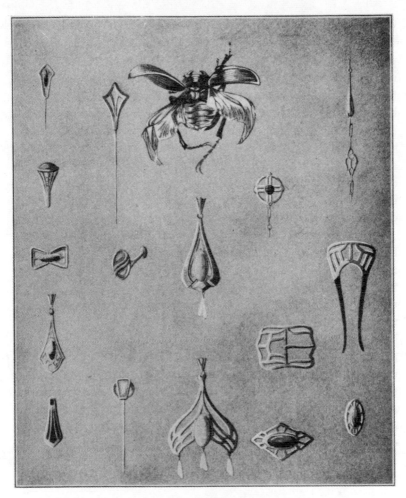

The designer with creative imagination reads into nature
endless possibilities for designs

when it was spread at the smaller end, as fig. M. The change modifies the background space and helps to create a pleasing pattern in the metal part. In fig. N, a unit was needed because it was felt that there was too much metal, the design looked heavy. The additional unit is seen in fig. N at O. The change lightens up the whole pattern which, as it is, may be pierced, enameled or chased. Whatever process is employed at this stage, the design has the appearance of being unfinished around the rim. A flat wire with nicks to relieve its plain effect or a line raised from the back seemed desirable to improve the design. The bezel can also be modified to carry out the floral idea if it is scalloped on the edge as in fig. N.

If this same design is to be chased, the motif should be modeled only slightly above the surface. This element may be used less conventionalized so that the identity of the flower is more distinguishable. The unit may be a little more than the silhouette used in the pierced design. It may contain the characteristic turn of the petals and some of the light and dark effects, and adapted to the flat surface of the metal in bas-relief. It should be remembered in designs of this kind that the more detail represented in a single unit the fewer the times the unit is to be repeated, and vice versa. Page 239 represents designs derived from a tendril. It will be noticed how the spiral stems have been used in varying proportions and modified to suit certain chosen shapes. This tendril is suggestive of many beautiful pieces of wire jewelry.

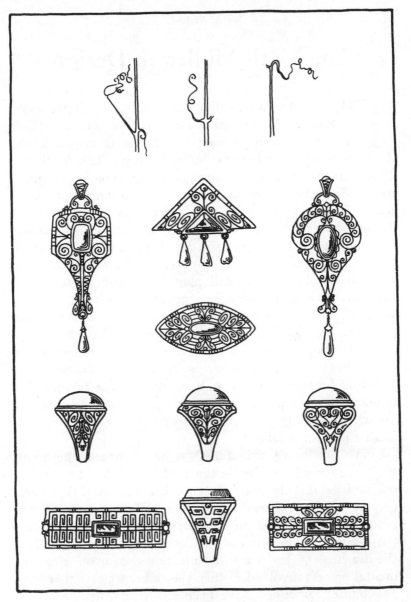

Even an ordinary bit of nature seen with imagination
suggests jewelry designs

CHAPTER 29

The Moth Mullen in Design

TO keep our work alive and full of spirit we must revert to Nature, the inexhaustible source. Plant life alone offers a vast storehouse from which the designer may draw inspiration and suggestions for ideas. Plants are endowed with shapes, forms, and colors that guide us in our endeavor to interpret them in terms of useful needs. The vast number of motifs that may be elicited from a single flower is beyond the conception of the untrained and at times is even amazing to the designer himself. Everything in nature, regardless of its importance, has a message for the trained observer. Small plants of insignificant size or color may stimulate the keen student of nature to produce wonderful results. Material which would not attract even a passing notice by the layman is often the incentive to beautiful and exquisite creations. But, as was intimated in the preceding chapter, whatever is used as motifs to create beautiful patterns must first pass through the imagination of man. This is a process of change, adjustment, adaptation, and elimination that the flower goes through before it realizes its final expression.

For our motif this time we have chosen the moth mullen, page 241. The designer who is quick to see the possibilities for ideas at a glance can record the changes necessary without drawing out the different steps of approach as represented on page 243. This thinking process that goes on in the mind of the designer is demonstrated by the drawings on the plate just mentioned to make clear the mental process involved. When the external parts that have possibilities for design have been recorded, when each part has been drawn from different points of view in order to give the most interesting aspects, we should go farther and look beneath the visible parts of the flower. We now seek to get

Study this illustration, then turn to the following pages
to see how the designer used the moth mullen

the beauty that lies hidden beneath the surface by folding over the leaves or by making sectional drawings of buds, flowers, and seed pods. The cutting may be done with a sharp knife by passing it longitudinally or transversely through the bud or whatever part of the plant is used. A careful examination of the result will reveal the mysterious way in which order manifests itself in nature. The drawings, as represented on page 243, at once suggest many ways of adaptation. The various parts of the plant were studied for an idealistic interpretation rather than for a realistic representation. To the student who is versed in the craft for which he is designing, such drawings open up a vast field of ideas. These drawings show the parts of the flower that appealed to this student, to another student the selections might have been entirely different or translated, perhaps, in a different temperament or mood. These may be reconstructed for jewelry according to the ability of the student to display them with fine proportions and dignified contours. The designer sees possibilities of using it first in various ways and to this end tries many schemes of arrangements. As far as the plant itself is concerned it may not be beautiful, but it is what the designer brings to it, in the way of knowledge as to how it may be adapted in terms of tool processes, that is responsible for the beauty attained after all. The designer creates beauty out of the material at hand regardless of its inherent qualities. He subjects the plant to many trials until some satisfactory arrangement or orderly design is brought out. The success of the result, however, depends entirely upon the ingenuity of the designer. He may ignore traditional methods and principles and achieve creations that defy the highest authorities, or he may use them in a formal or commonplace way and evoke only a casual commendation. By ingenious methods he may create works of art from the commonplace material. This ingenuity is a power in the individual which asserts itself in every line, every mass, and in every pencil or brush touch that the design possesses. The jewelry designs on page 245 have been derived from the

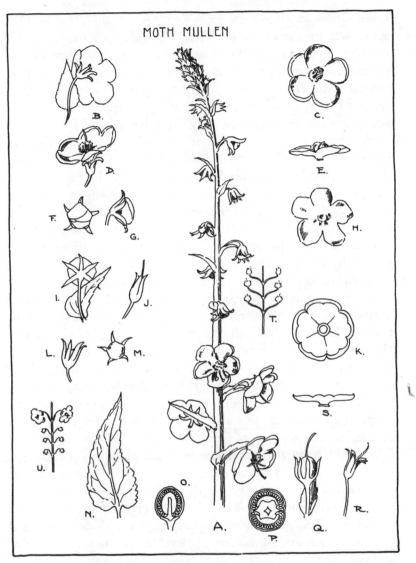

MOTH MULLEN

A graphic exposition of what the designer discovers when examining
nature's exquisite plant forms in terms of his needs

same flower as shown on page 243. A careful drawing of a spray was first made to become thoroughly acquainted with the flower. The steps of conventionalizing the flower and its parts have been omitted in this plate and only the designs represented. They show clearly the part of the plant that received the most attention and consequently the part adaptable for jewelry. The way these stems typify the shape of the stone, their downward or upward growth, deserves no little attention. The translation of flowers, leaves, and buds into metal and stone is made in a thoroughly clear and simple way, there is no confusion as to growth or arrangement; each part is related to each other and to the whole. The stones used have been made to harmonize with the quality of the design. It was deemed necessary from the very outset to make the designs depict the delicate nature of the plant. The rendering of these designs indicates the forms and relief, and consequently points to the technical process most desirable to reproduce them. During the designing process this was kept in mind and adhered to. We might reconstruct these same designs in terms of another method of producing them as by perforation or enameling. The method of execution plays an important part in the designing process.

The contour of the different designs, however, was not suggested by the plant or any part of it. They are simply the results of knowledge of jewelry shapes. The motif for decoration, however, was taken from the plant as is evidenced by the character of the designs. These motifs, flowers, buds, and leaves, were adapted to the shapes selected according to the arrangements described in the chapter on structural elements. The massing and grouping were done according to principles found in nature, as rhythm, balance, symmetry, and radiation. Rhythm is quite conspicuous in the small bud-like forms as they decrease or increase in size. Their arrangement around the stone accentuates the interest enough to make it the center of attraction. The lines of the brooches and pendants show the stems have been changed from straight lines to conform to the shape of the jewel desired.

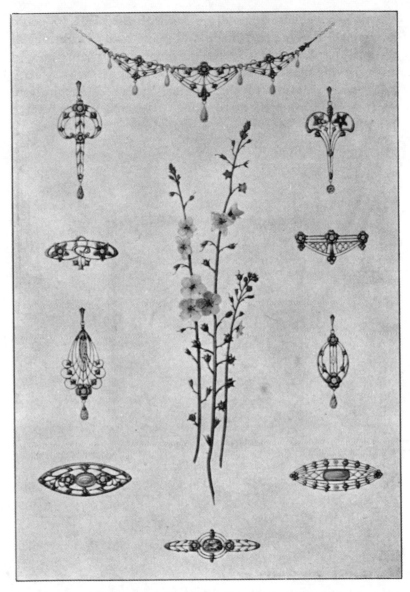

A few jewelry designs suggested by the moth mullen and created by the artist

When we have done all we can with the plant, we could turn to the designs just made and make many variations of them. After having made designs direct from nature and, in turn, having made variations of these designs, we may look back with pleasure to the original source of inspiration, Nature, with a heightened feeling of reverence and respect for her humble objects.

CHAPTER 30

The Snow Crystal in Design

A STUDY of the three vast kingdoms of nature, namely, the animal, vegetable, and mineral, leads us to adopt the Platonic theory that nature proceeds by geometry. This would convince us if we were to make careful microscopic examination of some of her small forms.

In this exercise we have taken the common snowflake that is so familiar. We know what beautiful effects the snow makes in winter as it covers the universe with its white mantle, but few of us have taken the trouble to study the minute and perfect geometrical structure of the evanescent snow crystals. These crystalline masses depend upon the degree of cold for the perfection of their geometric forms; the colder the atmosphere through which they fall, the more perfect are their forms. The drawings on page 249 indicate a few outline patterns from the handiwork of Nature, while the frontispiece, Book II, shows the modeling in detail. It is clear that their construction varies in design; this variation being due to a condition of the atmosphere other than that of temperature. But if the designer is not interested in the cause of their formation, his keen observation must be arrested by their wonderfully beautiful designs and by the ideas they may suggest. In no form of nature that we have studied thus far do we find shapes that approximate ready-made designs as do the snow crystals. If we were to take them literally and apply a stone in the center, an edge to give the outline a simpler contour, and proceed to represent it as pierced or enameled we would have, in most cases, a pleasing result. It gives us an appreciation of patterns made by nature. These crystals on page 249 are rather precise in their construction, hence we call the patterns geometric. They are not so intriguing as figures that are free and have less symmetry in their composition. But it is not necessary to take the crystal bodily and use it as was formerly suggested. We may concentrate on some one part of it and use the motif in any shape we may have in mind. This is much more difficult than repeating the same unit radially. The result has more artistic merit. This is clearly seen in the designs on the frontispiece, Book II. The crystal on this page has been partly rendered, giving its intricate pattern on the surface. The first idea that this crystal suggests is a hexagonal brooch, as is indicated by the hexagonal design. Upon examination, it will be seen how much this brooch design resembles the natural snow crystal in its composition; as some of the units are used bodily, the design is only informally conventionalized. The pearls filling in the angular spaces made by the diverging lines show how the designer is able to overcome unpleasant conditions in the parts that do not permit any change. It is a matter of bringing in knowledge of the jewelry craft to aid in improving such places. Note how this same design has been worked out in the elliptical-shaped brooch at the bottom of the plate. Here the same motif has been used, but instead of being identical in size, it has been varied to suit the shape chosen. It makes a more pleasing design, because there is more variety in size among its similar units. The pearls have not been used in the angles of the contour, since there are but four in number, using them would create four disconnected masses holding the eye in fixed positions. Note in this design how much more attraction the stone has, with its size increased, than in the hexagonal one. Note how the design has been greatly simplified, although compared in parts it has many shapes and masses in common with the natural form. The design in the upper right is suggested by the inner part of the crystal, by the white lines that cross each other and enclose dark small masses of various sizes. This spot appears six times around the crystal while here it is used but four. A circle was made and then these lines were drawn to radiate from four diametrically opposite points on the circumference. As the circle was simply for construction, it was erased and a four-pointed star, enclosing a circular stone, was made to take its place.

SNOW CRYSTALS
SUGGESTING PATTERNS FOR JEWELRY

The study of snowflakes suggests interesting natural patterns
for jewelry designs

The contour was simplified by adding metal areas between the four principal units. This necessitated the addition of other lines as well as the pearls. In the design under this one, it will be seen that the horizontal units at the extreme ends are similar to some in the crystals and to those used in the hexagonal design, although somewhat modified in their outlines. The vertical motif can easily be distinguished in the hexagonal one and its variation, namely the elliptical brooch. In this design, however, there are but two of these used on the vertical axis, the other parts of the design have been devised to make up a harmonious result. This design is conventionalized to a greater degree than those just described. The design to the left is a variation of the one in the upper right and has very little in common with the snow crystal itself. It will be seen that the method of making ideas from nature becomes more and more formally conventionalized as we proceed in the evolution of design.

It will be seen by these designs how feasible it is to get ideas from nature and, also, how convincing the principle of variation can be.

CHAPTER 31

The Sea Horse in Design

The sea horse can suggest jewelry designs

IT really matters little how elaborate a motif or how humble a natural form one may choose; in the hands of a designer the most pretentious and artistic designs may be evolved from very commonplace subject matter. The ability to evolve ideas from natural forms is contingent with one's intensity of perceptual capacity. Inventing designs is as if one were distilling natural forms for the sake of precipitating the most meaningful and significant features related to that form. From a practical point of view, putting it simply and succinctly, it is but nature conveniently dressed in the materials in which it is to be realized, metals, wood, clay, fabric, plastic, etc. in the manner of rhythms, balances, and harmonies. It is as if nature were passed through the alembic of the imagination, the latter being all inclusive of materials, their manipulative susceptibilities, and the orderly nature of design.

Nature stands ready to surrender to man her wealth of subject matter with all its mysteries. She leaves it for us to rearrange, modify and choose according to the dictates of our best thoughts, thus creating a nature all our own. Nature gives us the material from which it is possible to create beauty, but unless we approach her with a knowledge of the laws and principles of repetition, balance, rhythm and the skills to use these, our efforts will be in vain. It is within the province of design that the artist translates his orderly thoughts, a language of line, dark and light, and color into material things. For the purpose of demonstrating that it is an easy matter to evolve designs from the commonplace things in life, we have selected a sea horse (page 251), a subject not beautiful enough to arouse any contradiction.

This sea form, *Hippocampus Puntulatus*, performs no useful function, as an organism it has no usable qualification nor is it a collector's item. To the naturalist it is interesting only as a physical phenomenon, to the designer it is interesting because of its possibilities for ideas.

A few significant facts of its physical nature and ways of life can act as stimulation for designs in general and for jewelry needs in particular.

It is unique in certain physical qualities and modes of behavior. In general it is four inches long, has large eyes capable of flexible focusing powers, it resembles the horse in outline only and has a most fascinating chameleon-like coloration, it has a long prehensile tail and fast moving dorsal fins, its bodily markings are of geometric progressive patterns; on the habit side of behavior it reverses nature's order of rules and regulations for it is the only sea form that swims in a vertical position, it enjoys immunity from being devoured by other fish; besides its own power of locomotion, by means of its long tail, it can attach itself to other fish while in motion and enjoy a free ride.

The illustration on page 253 shows one article in which the sea horse has been used in a very informal way. The two sea horses here wind about each other as they often do in life. This arrangement was suggested by a study of the living subjects. This same arrangement, with a little stretching of the imagination, may be adapted to the shank of a ring as is represented by the cast shown at right in upper illustration, page 124. The treatment is rather naturalistic since there is but little modification in its form. When they were designed for the ring they passed through slight changes in order to conform to the peculiar shape of the ring shank. After the

Sea horse as
motif

sea horses were adjusted in place, an empty area was created between them that demanded due consideration. The motif to be used for such a space should bear some relation to the ornament already employed. The naturalistic treatment of the sea horse is well apparent so that whatever natural form is used it must also be conventionalized to the same degree. After some thought and search for a motif it was deemed wise to select something from the fish's natural environment and nothing seemed more appropriate than a seaweed. The seaweed motif was then drawn between the sea horses, allowing it to grow gradually from the base of the shank of the ring as though it grew out of it and to attain full growth between the fishes. Thus we have used this humble subject in a rather informal conventionalized manner, retaining to a large extent the character of its features and at the same time we have interpreted them in terms of metal as a means of decoration for the finger.

But this is not all that is possible with the sea horse. If we can think of it in its simplest form, merely its contour, and then simplify it still more, we can use it as a motif for repetition in a circle which, when arranged on the right and left of a stone, makes an attractive pin, page 256, fig. F.

The curl of the tail makes an excellent spiral and is easily applied to many forms of jewelry. If the spiral tail is accentuated, we find it will lend itself to many forms of jewelry, producing exquisite designs. This part constructs one of the vital curves that was mentioned in Chapter 25 and which is capable of so many applications. The stones chosen should be suggestive of the environment of the sea horse.

Careful study of the body discloses many interesting checkered shaped units. The rectangular shape figure, in which is inscribed a diamond, is repeated over the body in decreasing and increasing measures. Although each spot resembles the one above and the other one below, yet it varies to such an extent as to suggest a different idea or motif. In spite of its simple character this motif is used to demonstrate the possibilities of which it is capable. In the two rings on page 256 the idea can easily be traced back to the sea horse and be readily recognized. On examining this subject again we find this diamond shaped unit which apparently has very few possibilities for decoration. This motif, like the other, was not chosen because it seemed highly enriched with ideas but simply to demonstrate what is possible. Again, it was not chosen with the hope that it might fit any conventional jewelry shape; but the motif was adjusted to a particular article, in this case the elliptical brooch. It was planned to have the designs in wire with a number of stones. The diamond shape motif was modified in order to fit the shape of the brooch chosen. The motif can easily be recognized on page 256, fig. d, although there are many of them in an interlacing arrangement. In fig. c the rectangular shape has been modified so that it has assumed the shape of an oval. This can easily be distinguished at the right and left of the large elliptical stone. The diamond in the original rectangle has given way to lines that radiate from the extremities to the central stones. Half of the original diamond shape still remains while the other half has been converted into a double-branched volute curve holding a small circular stone. The circular brooch (fig. f) represents the sea horse highly conventionalized and simplified to such a degree as to retain only the contour. They have been clustered in pairs about a central faceted stone. As the problem was to be kept very light in its appearance and executed in round wire, the motif was translated with this in mind, hence the piercing in the sea horse unit. When arranged side by side a place for a small circular stone was formed between the heads of the fishes. When these units were placed on the vertical and horizontal axis, they seemed to leave much space between them, perhaps just enough to allow four more units. As it was deemed wise not to use these again in order to avoid monotony, it was necessary, therefore, to search for some unit that would fill the empty space and that would harmonize with the motif

already used. Such a motif might be suggested by or taken
from the units already in the design. The triangular shape
unit selected was suggested by the opening in the sea horse
already conventionalized. It has been made symmetrical
and the curly endings have given way to curves that blend
into the bezel of the stone. The finish, which appears at both
top and bottom of this triangular unit, gives it the appearance
of growing out of the brooch itself. Page 256, fig. e, is another
brooch of wire that has been evolved from the same motif,
although the conventionalization of the diamond shape motif
is very formal. The two lower bar pins (figs. g and h),
show how the same rectangular motif with the inscribed
diamond figure has assumed a geometric appearance. In
fig. g the rectangle is quite long, while the diamond is made
to fit the varied proportions. This unit by virtue of its proportions created a place for a gem stone. A circular stone
was chosen in preference to other shapes, in order to emphasize the long bar effect of the pin. As the rim was flat and
uninteresting it was enhanced by cutting away some of the
metal, thereby creating a dark and light effect recalling the
surface character of the sea horse. These spots are square in
shape, again keeping to the straight line character of the unit
chosen. Fig. h makes a very interesting bar pin. The diamond shapes have been subjected to such variation as to
create a motif which, when placed side by side, evolves semi-
circular shaped figures. The modified squares have been
filled with stones and alternating spirals thus carrying out
the curl of the sea horse. Interest has also been added by the
contrast of stones of different sizes.

Page 257 represents a number of designs derived from
various parts of the sea horse.

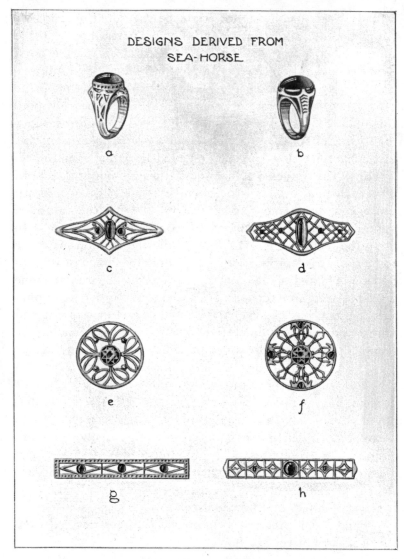

The markings on the sea horse suggest shapes and lines for
interesting designs

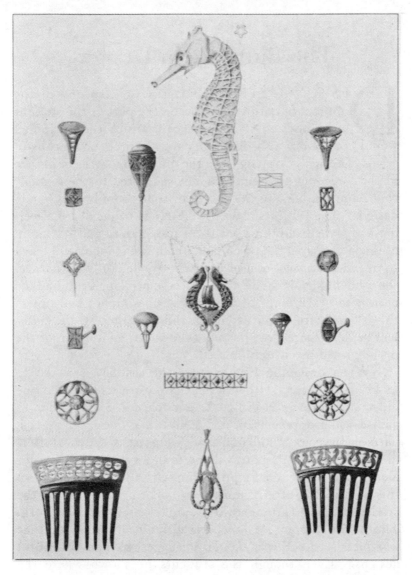

Jewelry designs derived from the sea horse

CHAPTER 32

The Butterfly in Design

DESIGNING from the butterfly or from any of the sources of nature involves on the part of the student not only ability to see motifs which the untrained would not see but also the ability to interpret such motifs in terms of design. Copying from the different sources of nature in the foregoing problems was not suggested to the student that he might hope in the course of time to find ready-made designs. The subjects chosen were given to inculcate a feeling of balance, rhythm, beautiful proportion, and harmony of line and shape, the principles which the student will learn to use in his production of designs. While studying nature, the student should strive to keep these principles in mind, or better, to make notes of them as he goes along; and unless this is done with active attention and real interest, the study will be done merely for its own sake and the vital aim of the problem will be entirely missed.

When designing from nature the student is asked to make an exact copy, either in pencil or brush, as shown by the illustrations (page 261, fig. A, and page 263), in order to gain a wider appreciation of its rhythmic lines and shapes, harmonious color, and balance or symmetry of spots. Butterflies with beautiful spots will be found very suggestive for ideas. The student may prove himself to be very skillful in this and yet be utterly unable to make up a design of the crudest sort even after shown examples and illustrated work. The novice cannot see how this insignificant weed or that worthless seed pod was enough to suggest so many beautiful designs. Even though the students be shown where the different designs came from, which part of the flower suggested this design and which that, they cannot make them unless a didactic method of instruction is offered.

Pages 261 and 262 show just the way the designer thinks when confronted with this problem. Page 261, fig. A is a very

Butterflies, a visual aid to stimulate ideas in jewelry design

careful pencil drawing of the butterfly, showing all detail. Fig. B shows a unit that apparently has possibilities of suggesting an idea. Fig. D shows that the unit has been simplified, thereby becoming a formal representation of this part of the fly. On page 262, fig. H still bears the characteristic features of fig. D, but with much more formality. The lines representing the ribs of the fly have been increased in number and the upward rhythmic movement has been accented. The rectangular spots at the ends of these lines have correspondingly been increased and modified to carry out the upward direction of the lines. The upper part of the body of the fly has given way to a stone while the lower part has been replaced by a drop. The head conveniently made way for three circles which might be granulations while the antennae are curled into involute curves around the three circles. The design thus far is in abstract terms, no thought having been given to the method of execution, the aim being first to produce an arrangement with no idea as to practicalities. Fig. J shows how such a composition of lines and masses can be reconstructed or interpreted in terms of metal and some definite process of execution. The result here attained is for a pierced brooch although it might have been made for enamel or even for the repoussé process.

Page 261, fig. C is another part of the same fly. Part of this was taken and reversion is resorted to as shown by fig. E. By this simple process of reversion we have created a series of lines radiating downward to left and right from a common axis. Familiarity with jewelry suggested a hanging of some kind, a pendant possibly. Hence on page 262, fig. I expresses the same downward effect of these lines with some modification of the ends and the spots between the lines. These lines created an open space and it was taken advantage of by inserting a stone that suggests its shape. The three drops were added to emphasize the downward effect of the pendant. This design, like page 262, fig. H, is merely in abstract terms. It is a cluster of lines radiating downward from a vertical axis. The design is now to be interpreted in terms of metal,

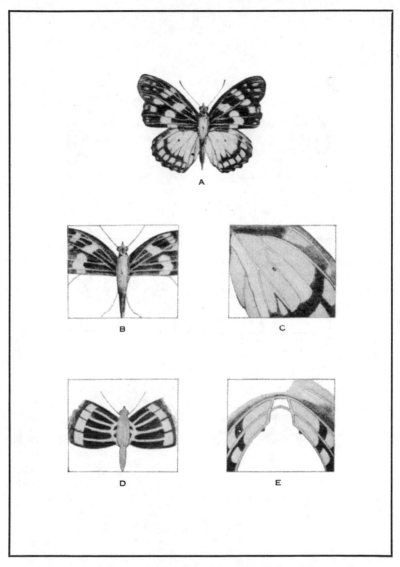

Sections of the butterfly enlarged, symmetrized and processed
in terms of design principles

Simple steps from the processed design principle to the finished design

Motif suggestions from enlarged details of the butterfly

Designs extracted from details of the butterfly

stones, and a tool process. Fig. K shows that it has been interpreted in fine wire. The spaces between the main lines of the design have been filled in with scrolls since they looked empty and unattractive. The other modifications and additions have been made to create a harmonious whole. The result is a total design for a jewel which the layman marvels at, wondering how unit B or C was the origin of that beautiful design. A collection of butterflies such as page 259 is invaluable for this kind of work. Page 263 shows studies made from a butterfly in this collection while on page 264 are a number of designs evolved from the butterfly.

The question may now arise as to whether it is necessary for the student to have some knowledge of the making of jewelry in order to design practical jewelry and do it with facility. Of course it would be of great help to know how the jewel is put together but it is not absolutely necessary. When the student has familiarized himself with jewelry processes, and has some creative ability, he should be able to produce good results.

When the student has grasped the method of attacking the problem, or better, the method of interpreting units for design, he is beginning to develop creative power that can evolve designs from almost anything. Just as soon as the student is able to look at any part or unit of the butterfly and see in it endless possibilities in design, he will never be hampered for ideas, he will see more possibilities in a single motif than ever before, and his pencil will not work fast enough to record these ideas.

If this method of designing is followed, the student will never be wanting in ideas. Designing from nature will render the ideas free from strain and overlabor; they will look fresh, possess a feeling that will tell that they were done with freedom and spontaneity.

CHAPTER 33

Designing the Elliptical Brooch

IN designing a brooch it is first necessary to ascertain the exact requirements and conditions. This brooch is to have a stone, cabochon preferred, and must have a design with perforations. Its dimensions may be arbitrary in length and breadth. The motif for ornamentation is to be abstract. The abstract motif may be arranged in many different ways but must be reduced to some tangible idea in order to solve the problem. It becomes necessary then to state it in more specific terms, such as motifs that are concentric or eccentric, or motifs radiating from the center along the vertical and horizontal diameters, or any other arrangement as suggested in the circles on pages 187 and 188. Some such conception of arrangement is necessary to create this design. The manner of breaking up the surface should be predetermined. The scheme should be clear in mind and adhered to. Suppose then that the surface is to be broken up by motifs that are concentric and are intercepted by vertical and horizontal lines. The first step is to sketch a number of ellipses of fine proportion, having in mind sizes that are suitable for brooches. Next draw the long and short diameters, and then inscribe a concentric ellipse of such diameters as to make fine space relations among the areas made by the curved and straight lines. It is well to draw enough ellipses to have ample chance for experimentation. When this is done, draw another ellipse in the center for a stone appropriate in size. In order to make the exercise as profitable as possible, the stones in each ellipse should vary from a small to a fairly large size. Up to this time we have been dealing with pure line, now it behooves us to realize what we have in terms of metal and stone. Instead of thinking of them as mere lines, think of them as bands of metal of various widths and draw them as such. When this is done it will be quite evident that we have a design, severely simple, nevertheless one fulfilling the requirements.

Good spacing will determine the success of these as well as other problems of more complexity. The design must display a fine adjustment of one perforation with another, of perforations and metal that embodies them. The intricacy of the pattern should increase with each design—instead of a single metal band radiating right and left, we might double them, creating more metal and more small spaces. Each metal band added creates additional light effect and consequently complicates the solution. But, regardless of the number of spaces created by the metal bands, the problem is one of dark and light, and its charm consists in its contrast of small and large areas of the right relationship. It must always be kept in mind that the real interest is attained in the metal and that whatever perforation is made must ultimately leave a fine pattern in the metal. These sketches should be made with spontaneous efforts without stopping to erase errors for modifications. When a result is not satisfactory, begin with a new ellipse. There should be no hesitating efforts; every stroke should be the direct result of a convincing thought. The good designs in turn might be perfected by the use of tracing paper. This method is advocated so as to keep the original design intact. The perforation may be modified so as to assume more shape and character. This is accomplished by adding a line or area here and there which influences the shape of the metal in which we are primarily interested.

Illustrations on page 25 represent a number of designs constructed on structural elements of various types to show some good examples of pierced elliptical brooches. It should be noticed in these designs that the success is due to a fine relation between the length and breadth of the ellipse, to the proper relation of openings and metal, to an agreeable contrast of small and large openings, and to the unity and simplicity of the idea expressed.

Large simple masses in contrast with clusters of striated
areas give interesting modern effects

CHAPTER 34

Buckles, Clasps, and Bar Pins

THE buckle is made of one or two strong pieces of metal, usually with a pin placed horizontally across to be inserted into the ribbon or belt. Buckles are also used for shoes, with a narrow strip of metal on the under side to which the ribbon may be sewed. The pin originally used to fasten the belt has remained soldered on to the upper surface as a mark of tradition, performing no particular function, but lending an artistic effect.

Oftentimes this device, when used on a belt, is made of two distinct pieces, one placed at either end of the ribbon. The piece at the right end of the belt having a hook, while the other has a slot. This kind of buckle is called a clasp (see above). In either case, the designer must take into consideration that there is a horizontal pull to overcome and consequently must meet this condition with metal strong enough to withstand the strain. The fact that it comes in contact with parts of the garment makes a simple outline imperative. It must be free from points or edges that will cause unnecessary wear and tear, hence the simple outlines on pages 269 and 270. The size may vary to suit the fancy of the designer or it may be governed by the particular belt it is to serve. The contour should be a simple rectangle, square or oval, or a slight modification of these, the surface may be enriched by an etched, chased, enameled, pierced, or appliqué design, keeping it always in low relief. Large cabochon

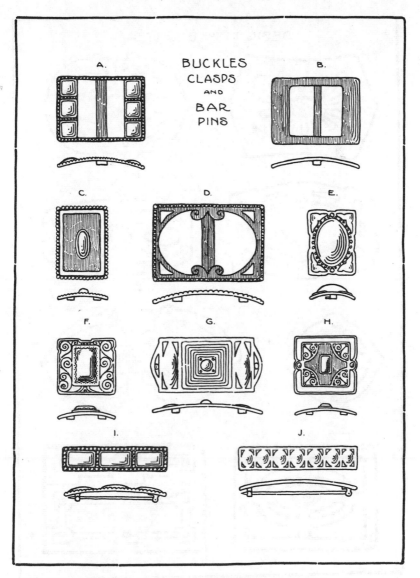

Buckles, clasps, and bar pins derive their design considerations
from the nature of their function

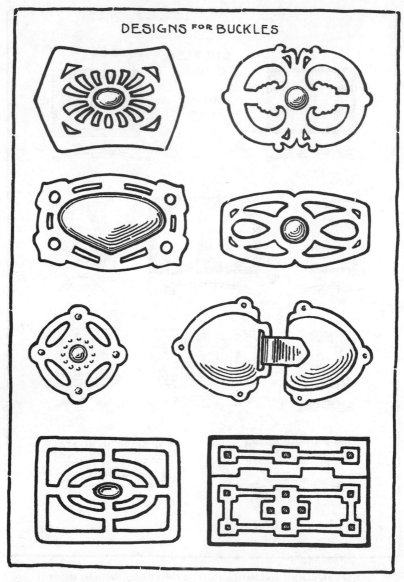

DESIGNS FOR BUCKLES

The possibilities for surface treatment to enhance the beauty of the buckle are many. Strength and massiveness is within its structure

Buckle designs with similar motifs using different contours

stones, as figs. E and F on page 269, with a small border design around them or even fancy wire, make pleasing and serviceable designs. The catch and the clasp of this problem are placed on the back. Such parts should be concealed whenever it is possible to do so and should not project very much above the surface of the buckle, as the latter in turn will protrude too much from the belt. With the foregoing facts embracing the function, limitations and possibilities of the article, the design confines itself to limitations which, instead of being a hindrance to the designer as might seem at first, are indeed, a help to the solution.

The bar pin is much the same as the brooch and buckle both in design and construction, the only difference is in its length and width. The bar pin being used horizontally has a dominant horizontal axis hence the outline and whatever ornament used should emphasize this effect. Fig. I, page 269, consisting of three rectangular stones with beaded wire around them and about the edge of the pin, carries out the idea above mentioned. Fig. J, however, at first glance seems to contradict the principle governing the bar pin. The units possess a dominant vertical axis, but these units are so short and so simple in their effect that the long horizontal effect of the pin itself is not disturbed.

CHAPTER 35

Pendant, Lavaliere, and Necklace

THE pendant is an ornament that is suspended from the neck by a chain. Its size varies to suit the wearer and it is usually worn over the garment. Another form of pendant, smaller and more delicate in character, is sometime in vogue, namely, the lavaliere. This is worn, almost without exception, with a low neck dress and is often set with a small brilliant. It is sometimes worn about the throat. Whatever the distinction, they are both types of pendants and are governed by the same principles of design.

The pendant may be arbitrary in its size and set with one or more stones of varying dimensions. The pendant idea must be set forth in a conspicuous way as the dominant characteristic in the design. This is done by emphasizing the vertical axis. The ornament used in conjunction with the stone, whether applied, carved, pierced, or enameled, should be consistent with the qualities of the stone or stones. A common shape for a pendant or lavaliere is pear or oval. The widest part may be above or below the vertical middle point as examples shown on page 273, figs. A, B, F, H. Other contours used are the ellipse, rectangle, diamond shape and circle. Whatever the shape, the stone or stones should form the center of interest and should, therefore, assume an important position on the pendant. When one stone is used, it is often more interesting to place it a little above or below the central point of the pendant. The examples of pendants just mentioned represent typical outlines and some structural elements upon which ornament may be invited.

Page 273, fig. A shows the use of the curves of force and grace, radiating from a common point on the upper side of the stone to form the contour of the pendant and terminating into scrolls on the inside and on the outside of the oval shape. The smaller scrolls at the bottom of the pendant grow out of

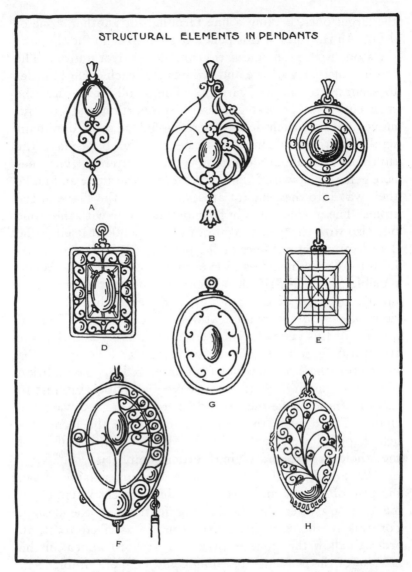

STRUCTURAL ELEMENTS IN PENDANTS

Constructing the design with the stone as the principal center of interest

the larger ones, making a fine terminal for another stone or drop. All the lines of this pendant seem to echo the shape of the stone with pronounced rhythm and perfect unison. The scrolls must vary in size and grow out of each other in order to secure interest and variety. The scrolls must describe such curves as possess fineness of proportion and graceful movement. In each design there should be some dominant scroll effecting a definite movement. Fig. B displays the rhythmic lines about a common center of interest. The lines here generate upward from the bottom of the stone and make their way into the pendant area, embracing the shape of the stone. The movement is in harmony not only with the stone but also with the general contour of the pendant itself. The dominant structural lines of the pendant lead the eye grace-fully to the chain slide and eventually to the chain. When possible, the chain should appear to emerge gracefully and tangentially out of the pendant, and never abruptly or at right angles to the main features of it. The ornamental interest of this pendant has been intensified by allowing the structural lines to terminate in leaves and florets. The interest of the stone has not been impaired by the addition of these forms since some of the leaves carry their interest to it, while those above the stone deliberately move toward the chain. The drop in this pendant has taken the form of a bell-shaped flower, conforming to the naturalistic effect of the whole design, and giving vertical emphasis.

Page 273, fig. C is a pendant showing a large stone. Because of its size and color, it is deliberately intended to make its qualities the dominating features of the design. For this reason very little ornament is ascribed to it, in order to allow the stone to make the greatest appeal in the interest of the pendant. Nothing could be more simple than plain bands of circular wire interrupted at various places with silver shot to relieve the simplicity.

Fig. D illustrates the way in which it is possible to adapt elliptical and circular stones to a rectangular contour. The corners have been rounded to soften the angularity. The main

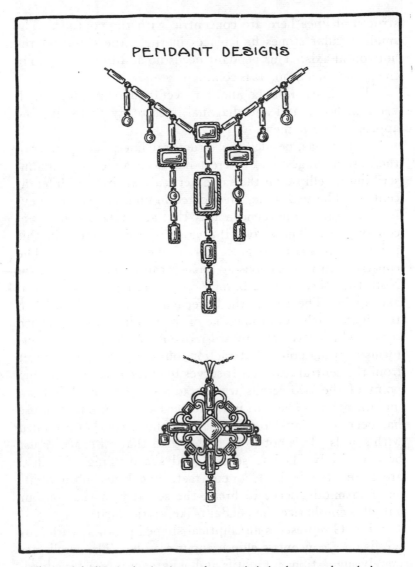

PENDANT DESIGNS

The straight line is the dominant characteristic in these pendant designs

structural lines here are concentric with the contour. The small circular stones find places in the corners and on the horizontal axis. This pendant needs no additional feature in the nature of a drop. It is complete.

Fig. E represents another rectangular pendant with vertical, horizontal and diagonal lines ready to receive the appropriate ornament.

Fig. F has, besides the structural lines, one quarter of the design suggested. Interest has been added by circumscribing an ellipse on the same vertical axis but on different centers. The two stones are located in unusual places relieving the design from the formality that accompanies the usual conventions. The scrolls that form the decoration in this pendant are made to grow out of the vertical axis. The construction is analogous to most forms of natural growth. Note that these scrolls branch out, meeting at the vertical axis again. The area in the lower half of the two ellipses on the right which form the frame of the pendant are filled with scrolls which have an upward movement. The round stone forms a strong point of attraction, but not enough to detract from the central feature. It serves to emphasize the meeting point of the two scrolls which radiate right and left from underneath it. The area in the lower half of the small ellipse has been left blank to contrast with the parts that are filled with scrolls. It is not to be understood that all spaces must be completely filled to secure good space filling. Unfilled areas are often desirable for contrast. The drops on the right, left and middle serve to break the severity of the contour and also emphasize the pendant-like verticularity.

Fig. G represents an elliptical-shaped pendant with four scrolls on a concentric ellipse about a stone. The scrolls are merely suggestions for motifs and, whatever interest is added, should resemble the first thought and harmonize with it.

Fig. H is similar in contour to fig. F but the oval in this case has been filled unsymmetrically. Although the scrolls radiate right and left into the oval area there is an occult balance that is unusual, and pleasing to the eye. The stone

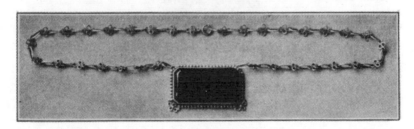

Students' jewelry based on distinctive designs

is the center of interest but is not placed in the center of the pendant. It serves at this place as a point from which the scrolls may radiate. The small end of the pendant below the stone is made more interesting by working the metal into small ornamental units, thereby relieving the stone from an otherwise heavy appearance acquired by its location. The method of distributing the ornament is less conventional than those previously described, but much more interesting.

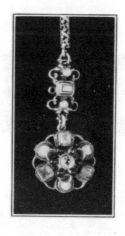

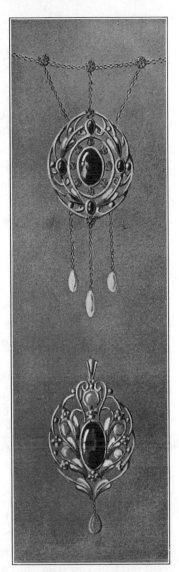

Precious stones and
metal in perfect union

Pendant designs showing
downward movement

CHAPTER 36

The Finger Ring

HISTORY tells us that wearing rings was probably introduced into Greece from Asia, and into Italy from Greece. Unlike today, in ancient times they served a two-fold purpose, ornamental and useful, being employed as a key or a seal, the latter being called "sphragis," a name given to the gem or stone on which figures were engraved.

Long ago both sexes wore rings in profusion. At the close of the 18th century enormous rings were worn. The hand of a woman presented a good collection of rings. During this period the wedding ring was unnoticed on the fingers of women, being almost completely concealed by other wide and ornate rings. So important was ring production, therefore, that its manufacture was separated from the ordinary work of the goldsmith and was made, thereby, a trade in itself.

Today, as an ornament, the finger ring is the most common form of jewelry. The design is limited in shape and area. All rings have a point of attraction either in the stone or in the decoration, the wedding ring alone being an exception. The ring form is a device to display a stone which in turn adorns the finger. This fact makes the stone the main point of interest in this form of jewelry. Some of the Egyptian and Roman rings, consisting of plain bands of metal set with roughly cut stones with extremely little if any ornament, illustrate this point. As in all forms of design the ring must comply with the principle of fitness to purpose. The part of the ring that is on the inside of the finger must be narrow enough to cause no discomfort to the wearer while the top of the ring may be light or heavy as desired. The lines forming the sides of the shank should be simple curves, admitting slight modification. When ornament is used it should be subordinated to the stone and all other interest

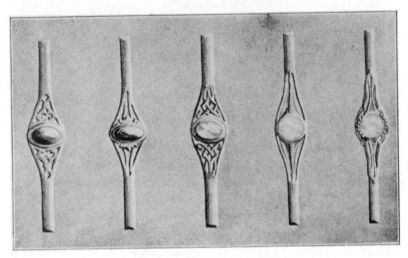

Finger rings designed in the blank

added as decoration should lead the attention from the shank up to the stone, if there is one, in a graceful manner with ingratiating effect. The stone should be the center of interest while the decoration on the shank and around the stone might well reflect its character. If the stone is light and delicate in color the design of the ring and the decoration should be in harmony with these qualities. The stone forming part of the metal band should be thought of as such in the process of designing. The method of setting it whether by prongs, gypsy, belcher, or in a box is determined by the nature and cut of the stone. A small stone of brilliant color can be made important if set in prongs, while soft stones may be set down into the metal in a gypsy setting, to protect the stone. Large and high stones should be set in elevation so that the gem and the ring assume a mirthful, sportive air.

Illustrations on page 82 represent designs that can be executed by the amateur craftsman. The simplest modification of the plain band would be two or more saw-piercings on the shank, increasing in width as they approach the stone.

Variations of these piercings should keep the vertical effect of the ring. Illustration on page 281 shows designs for casting and chasing. The same principles of design are involved here as in the pierced ring. We have in the first three designs an attempt to extol the qualities of the stone. The decoration is restrained and simple, neither overdone nor detracting from the interest of the gem.

Platinum rings present a charm that is all their own. The color, hardness and rarity of platinum restricts its use. Hence, instead of the synthetic method of building on the ornament, or by carving, it is preferable from the cost standpoint to produce the design by perforation. Hence the very fine saw-piercings impart the effect of delicate wire work. When designing a platinum ring as those illustrated on the opposite page, it should be treated much the same as fine wire work.

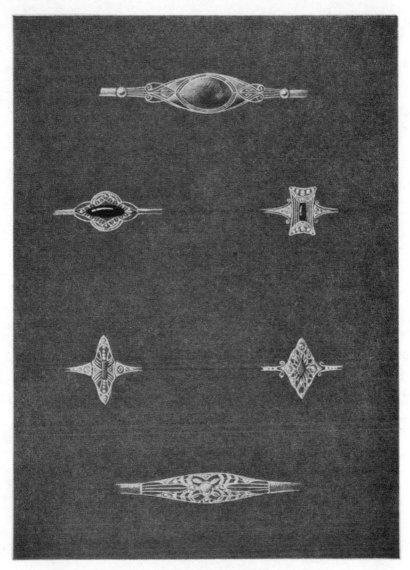

Platinum bracelets and rings designed with extreme delicacy

A leaf, a scroll, a few stones, skillfully and harmoniously arranged

CHAPTER 37

The Cuff Link and Cuff Button

AS was mentioned in the chapter on the principles of jewelry design, the cuff button or cuff link is one of the pieces of jewelry that may be called useful. It serves to keep the ends of the cuffs together. Cuff links may be made on the principle of a link with a loose disc on either end. Sometimes a button is duplicated on either end of a stem but it often has a bean at one end. The stem is curved in order that the cuff may come together when the button is in place. The use to which the cuff link is put determines the nature of its ornament and its contour. In order that it may be serviceable, it must be easy to insert into the cuff. This demands that the shape be of a convenient size and the ornament in low relief. If the button is used with a bean, it may be spherical or lentil shaped. The button may be made any shape so long as its outline remains unbroken. The shapes preferable for this purpose are rectangular, circular and elliptical. The elliptical designs on pages 284 and 287 are variations of the same idea. The designs herewith illustrated are curves which harmonize with the outline of the button. The design may be executed in a number of different ways; it may be etched, chased, or enameled. Those illustrated are designed for enamel as this is an attractive medium for artistic expression. The rectangular shaped designs on page 285 are also for cuff links or cuff buttons. This problem is simply the breaking up of a rectangular space. Whatever the problem, the technical process of execution should be foremost in the designer's mind, since in many ways it determines the nature and the structure of the design. It will be noted by the surface decoration in some of these designs that the patterns are impossible for pierced work, but may do very well for other technical processes. These illustrated are best adapted to enamel and are designed to be executed in that medium. The design is

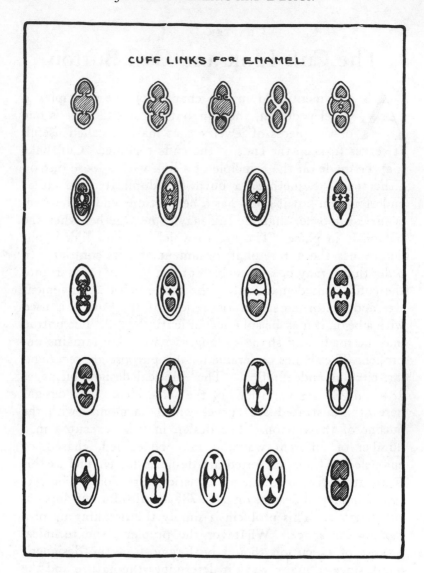

CUFF LINKS FOR ENAMEL

thought of in terms of channels that are to be cut out of the
metal to receive the enamel. These channels may be of various widths but the pattern is determined by the outline of the
button. The simplest design would be a repetition concentric
with the outline. A modification of this may be made by the
addition of another small concentric spot, again repeating the
shape of the outline. Further developments of the first idea
may be made by modifying the outline to a slight degree.

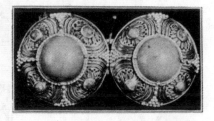

CUFF LINKS FOR ENAMEL

CHAPTER 38

Jewelry Coloring

DESIGNS rendered in color can show the kind of finish a piece of jewelry is to have, indicating whether it is to be finished in white, yellow, green or Roman gold, or matted, sand-blasted, or oxidized silver. These shades of color are determined by the designer after a careful study of the color of the stone which is to be mounted. It is important, therefore, that the designer have some knowledge of the colors that can be obtained with chemicals in order that he may use them and design intelligently.

The natural oxidation of silver is due to the presence of sulphur in the atmosphere. This very desirable color may be produced on silver by the use of chemicals in a very short time, with the following solution: one ounce of potassium sulphide to one quart of water. The solution is prepared by bringing the water to a boil, then dropping the sulphide in and allowing it to dissolve. The liquid is more effective if applied with a brush to the metal when warm, after the metal has been thoroughly cleaned. It is best to use a weak solution so that the oxidizing may be produced gradually. The piece of work may also be submerged into the solution until the desired color is produced, but if it has a stone that is comparatively soft, it will absorb the solution to such an extent as to ruin it. It is therefore best to apply the solution with a brush. When it has dried, sprinkle a little pumice powder over the work and brush it with a stiff brush until the desired shade of gray is obtained. If the color rubs off too easily, it shows that the solution was too concentrated and if light and dark spots appear with an uneven appearance, it shows that the work was not thoroughly cleaned before the solution was applied. The color may also be rubbed off the high places by taking a little moist pumice powder on the end of the thumb and working over it till the desired effect is obtained. It is then rinsed, and when dry, rubbed briskly with a cotton flannel or a chamois cloth. The high places should have a bright polish and if more polish than that obtained by the pumice is desired, a powdered rouge or a hand-buff may be used or, if a polishing lathe is at hand, rub stick rouge on the cotton or felt buff, and polish, being careful not to wear away the high points in the piece of work. Acid solutions used for coloring are best kept in enameled or earthen jars.

Silver jewelry may also be oxidized by using the following preparation: eighteen parts of graphite and three parts of powdered blood-stone mixed with either oil or turpentine. After the piece of work is dry, it is rubbed with a soft brush which is occasionally drawn over wax.

A blue-black color may be produced by using sulphide of ammonium and warming the object slightly till the desired shade of blue-black appears. It is then submerged in lukewarm soapy water, after which it is rubbed with a soft brush.

A pleasing brown may be produced by using the following: ten parts of sal-ammoniac, ten parts of blue vitriol and five parts of saltpeter mixed together.

For a rich ebony black use one ounce of chloride of platinum to a gallon of water; tellurium chloride may be used instead with equally good effect. DuPont's Darsil gives a most satisfactory black at less expense than either of the two chemicals.

Green oxidation may be produced by applying the following solution: three parts hydrochloric acid, one part iodine, one part water. When enough has been applied, that is, when the required color is reached, it is thoroughly rinsed and well dried. If possible, the piece of work should be left in the solution till the desired color is obtained. If the piece of jewelry has much relief work, the high places may be rubbed and polished, and then the green oxide may be again applied in the low parts only, until a beautiful green color is the result.

Polishing powder for jewelry may be made by mixing fifteen parts oxide of iron, eighty-six parts of carbonate of magnesia, and twenty parts of washed American Tripoli.

CHAPTER 39

Keeping Freshness in Your Work

THIS has to do with bringing forth fresh ideas habitually. Ideas come from the imagination. Imagining is building in the mind. The need for the desired thing is not there in the mind but brought in from the outside and suitably dressed. The influence for ideas is of two kinds, of Nature or of Geometry.

The first exists in natural forms, animal, mineral and vegetable; it is nature itself. The second is geometric in character, lines, areas, and solids. It helps to give shapes and forms to things in general. Ideas for jewelry must come from either of these two sources, there are no others.

An idea for a piece of jewelry is put together by rhythms, balances, and repetitions. These three, which design theory calls principles, are made evident by way of natural materials, stones, metals, and enamels. When such materials are fashioned, assembled, and harmoniously tied together, success is assured. It is an invention. The process is simple to understand and easy to achieve if certain design habits are cultivated in early training.

Habits in designing are like those in other forms of life. They are direct reports of thinking in terms of design principles and material to be used. The character of design, and workmanship too, are easily recognized because of obvious repetition. Repetition, however, can become deadening and lead to monotony. The basic causes for tired designs, over-labored ideas, and deadly sameness can be summed up in the lack of new approaches, a dearth of new motifs, and a marked hesitation to break with established routine. The ways of avoiding sameness of ideas, techniques and fixed mannerisms are important if joy in your work is to be maintained and freshness of ideas desired. The way is easy; the method —simple.

If ideas are added to the already vast existing designs in many forms, styles, and purposes which can be derived from nature and geometry, they will encourage new avenues of approach and creations. True, existing designs are historical, but what is there in the world that is not? Efforts that have contact with nature, geometry and the existing world of designs can set forth an endless source of new ideas. Ideas do not spring from the inner mind without the mind having first been affected by outside experience. Many contacts with nature, geometry, and the recording of these designs in a notebook is a habit worthy of cultivation. Nature with its boundless forms, shapes, masses, colors, all suggesting rhythms, balances and harmonies should be invading the notebook sometime each day.

But more important than building a storehouse of ideas—from nature and man-made things, a collection of related books, magazines, charts, drawings, in general, a working library—is your mental attitude toward the world of things. The designer, if creativity is to be cultivated as a way of life, must acquire the habit of seeing things in terms of his needs as of that moment. His mind should be sensitized to the things about him so that all things are seen and gracefully translated in terms of metals, stones, enamels, and design principles easily and convincingly.

CHAPTER 40

The Notebook

MANY times, the art student who is open minded, sees things in nature that inspire him to action; at other times, as he sits by himself dreaming of things beautiful, fleeting ideas come to him that may be startling. These moments, filled with thrilling beauty that excite the artistic impulse should be recorded, else they be gone never to return. It is this idea, this inspiration, that comes to us while our mind is unconsciously at play with the artistic Muse that later may serve as the incentive to a work of art. The ideas which are but imaginary in the beginning should be given visible interpretation. At these particular moments the notebook is invaluable. There are many beautiful motifs around us that can help in our work, but unless they are recorded and contemplated they will mean little or nothing, and we shall possess only a meagre storehouse of ideas. This is one of the ways that the student can gain an abundance of material as a storehouse of ideas. The notebook ought to be the student's constant companion since he may have occasion to use it at every waking hour. Sometimes it may be the little wild flower in the field, or the line of the creeping vine or, perhaps, the beautiful shape of the alderberry; and maybe the beautiful pattern made by the shadow of the big tree by our house, anything worth making note of. But let us not stop here; if we look toward the open sky, it may be the shapes of the little clouds as they appear over the horizon in rhythmic rolling procession; then the beautiful lines made by the smoke of the old farmhouse chimney is perhaps interesting with its long sweeping curves as it drifts upward and away. Then, too, while our eyes are still in the heavens, we note the line made by the swallows as they are soaring side by side. There are so many things that might be mentioned. The winter with its Jack Frost patterns on the window panes as we awake early in the

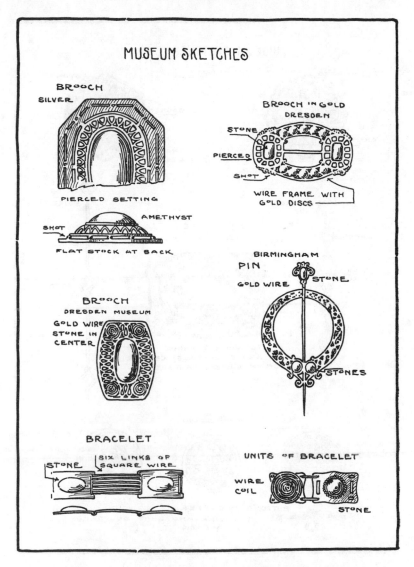

A visit to the jewelry collection of a museum rewards the student with many design suggestions

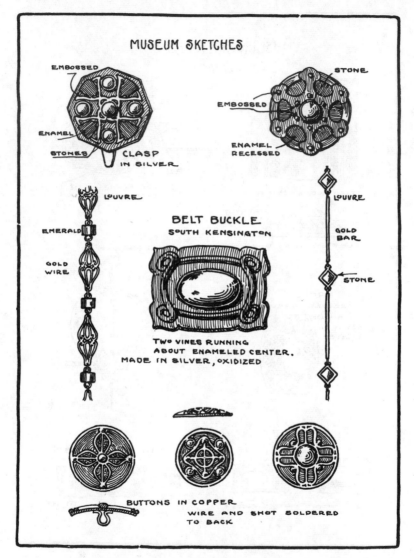

Descriptive notes accompanied by jewelry sketches help
recall design details for future use

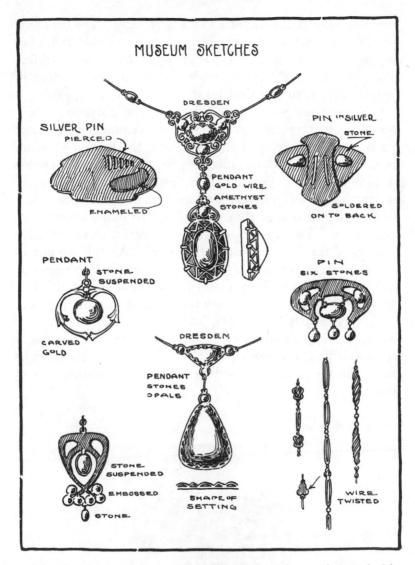

Plans, elevations, and cross sections of museum jewelry supplemented with descriptive notes make permanent records for future reference

morning may strike us with awe and wonder. The drooping icicles from the twigs of the lofty elm after a cold rain may suggest so much with their rhythmic curves, or sparkling glassy beads on the frozen buds may excite the student of jewelry design to practical ideas.

Then when going to the museum the notebook fulfills another great service and one which reminds us in later years of our visit to the Louvre of Paris, the British Museum in London, or the Metropolitan of New York. It will enable us to live again the joy we had in viewing the beautiful works of art, those which interested us most and arrested our attention to such a degree that we stopped to make a note here and there. Perhaps it was the wonderful hand-wrought jewelry of the Egyptian or of the Greek. All this we find in our precious notebook. The note may be no more than one quarter of a bilaterally symmetrical design as this is sufficient to recall the whole. Then with the aid of words and enlarged details as on pages 293, 294, and 295, the note means still more, so that should we feel at any time like making a replica, it would be quite possible to do so. The illustrations show the methods of recording notes of interesting bits of jewelry.

Setting and stone in perfect harmony

Reference Books

JEWELRY MAKING

CREATING JEWELRY FOR FUN, Andrew Dragunas. 146 pp. Harper and Brothers
  A manual on the techniques of creating handmade jewelry. The text, with over fifty diagrams demonstrating tools and how to handle them, and thirty photographs showing jewelry designs complete this book for the beginner.

HANDMADE JEWELRY, Wiener. D. Van Nostrand Company
  A manual illustrated with line drawings and photographs emphasizing the techniques in the making of jewelry.

HAND-WROUGHT JEWELRY, Sorenson-Vaughan. 102 pp. Bruce Publishing Company
  In twelve chapters hand-wrought jewelry is taken up from the simple to more complex types. The various operations such as piercing, sawing, oxidizing, soldering, carving, etc., are treated in simple manner.

HOW TO MAKE JEWELRY, George Overton. 55 chapters. Walter B. Frost Co.
  Written for the manufacturer, supplemented with illustrations. Chapters on the making of plated jewelry.

JEWELRY AND ENAMELING, G. Pack. D. Van Nostrand Company
  The technical processes of jewelry making and construction; a work manual for teachers and students. An excellent treatise fulfilling many requirements of this craft.

JEWELRY, GEM CUTTING AND METALCRAFT, W. T. Baxter. McGraw-Hill Publishing Co.
  A textbook for the student and home craftsman.

METALCRAFT AND JEWELRY, E. K. Kronquist. Manual Arts Press
  Photographs, drawings and instructions for making rings and other jewelry, as well as basic forms in metal.

NOTES ON JEWELRY AND METALWORK, Erma B. Hewitt. 62 pp. Alfred Press
  Some intimate recordings of processes, tools, materials, etc., in sequence of operations.

SMALL JEWELRY, F. R. Smith. Pitman Publishing Corporation
  Detailed explanation of methods of working with silver wire, sheet silver and stone setting.

SILVERWORK AND JEWELRY, H. Wilson
  A textbook of workshop practice in the precious metals.

UNIT JEWELRY, R. L. B. Rathbone
  A clear account of the designing and the construction of jewelry by the selection and assembling of small separate pieces or units.

JEWELRY DESIGN

APPLIED DESIGN IN THE PRECIOUS METALS, P. Wylie Davidson.   143 pp.
Longmans, Green & Co.
> This book stresses the need for good design in good workmanship.
> Emphasis on design and the results effected by the tools used on precious metals give this book a needed place in the craftsman's library.

LA BIJOUTERIE FRANCAISE, AU XIX E SIECLE, H. Vever
> Profusely illustrated with good reproductions of 19th Century French Jewelry.

ELEMENTS DE BIJOUTERIE ET DE JOAILLERIE MODERNES ET ANCIENS,
C. Scheedhauer
> Color plates of nineteenth century and early twentieth century jewelry in great variety.

JEWELRY, E. Basserman-Jordan
> Excellent illustrations of historic jewelry from the Bronze Age through eighteenth century.

JEWELRY, H. Clifford-Smith. 370 pp.   Methuen and Company
> Designing, as it fits the needs of the jeweler, is clearly explained with photographs and line cuts.

JEWELRY DESIGNS, Y. F. Jossic, Ed.
> Photographic reproductions of antiques, primitive and modern jewelry presenting a variety of patterns of every type.

STYLES OF ORNAMENT, Alexander Speltz.   Grosset & Dunlap
> Once referred to as the designer's Bible. Four hundred full-page illustrations with text and index according to subject and material.

VOLKERSCHMUCK OR PEOPLES JEWELRY
> A folio of 100 plates of primitive and antique jewelry. Suggests many ideas for jewelry designing.   •

ENAMELING

ENAMELING, Lewis F. Day. 22 pp.   B. T. Batsford
> The history and practice of the art of enameling from early times for the research student and for the student seeking practical information. Fully illustrated.

ENAMELING AND CHASING, Alexander Fisher
> Explains the technical processes employed in the various types of enameling, with chapters on miniature painting on metal.

HOW TO ENAMEL, Howard M. Chapin. 69 pp.   John Wiley & Sons
> A treatise on practical enameling of jewelry with hard enamels. A technical treatise, setting forth various processes such as charging, firing, stoning, preparing the enamel, are concisely told in an understandable manner.

METALWORK AND ENAMELING, Herbert Maryon. 317 pp.   Chapman and
Hall, Ltd.
>   Enameling, its processes and tools used, the various kinds of suitable
>   metal for enameling are all amply covered in this excellent volume.

PREPARATION OF THE PRECIOUS AND OTHER METALWORK FOR ENAMELING,
THE, D. De Konigh
>   An exposition of the processes and materials used by enamelers of the
>   past and the present.

THEORY AND PRACTICE OF ART ENAMELING, ON THE, H. H. Cunnynghame
>   A brief history of the craft of enameling and a practical explanation of
>   its execution in recent times.

CASTING

MOLDING AND CASTING, C. D. Clarke
>   A most comprehensive book on the subject, useful to jewelry craftsmen
>   and others.

CHASING AND REPOUSSÉ

REPOUSSÉ METALWORK, A. C. Horth
>   A manual for beginning craftsmen, giving a detailed listing of the tools,
>   materials and methods to be used.

ART METALRY

ART CRAFTING IN METAL FOR AMATEURS, F. Alexander
>   Discusses materials, tools and methods used in repoussé, chasing and
>   pierced work.

ART METALWORK, E. K. Kronquist. McGraw-Hill Book Company
>   Amply illustrated textbook by experienced commercial craftsman and
>   teacher.

ART METALCRAFT, A. F. Payne. Manual Arts Press
>   A complete introduction to tools and processes, illustrated by photo-
>   graphs and working drawings of objects made by a master craftsman.

ARTISTIC METALWORK, A. F. Bick. Bruce Publishing Company
>   Presents artistic but inexpensive projects for school and home with
>   limited equipment.

COPPER WORK, Augustus F. Rose. Metal Crafts Supply Company
>   A complete and comprehensive treatise offered in simple and didactic
>   form. Processes, tools, and projects fully covered.

ESSENTIALS OF METALWORKING, Edward Berg and Bristol E. Wing. 160 pp.
Manual Arts Press
>   Principles and processes about things in metal. Equipment, tools, and
>   machinery described and illustrated.

METAL ARTCRAFT, Thompson. D. Van Nostrand Company

MODERN METAL CRAFT, J. L. Feirer. Manual Arts Press
Gives detailed direction for metal projects.

ORNAMENT AND DESIGN

ARTS AND CRAFTS OF ANCIENT EGYPT, THE, W. W. Flinders. Petrie
Several chapters on metalwork and jewelry, enlightening and instructive.

CYCLOPAEDIA OF ORNAMENTS, F. Knight
Useful to jewelers, die sinkers, engravers and chasers.

ENCYCLOPEDIE ARTISTIQUE ET DOCUMENTAIRE DE LA PLANTE, M. P. Verneul
An analysis of floral forms applicable to design.

HANDBOOK OF ORNAMENT, Franz Sales Meyer. 580 pp. Hessling & Spielmeyer
Invaluable to the student of design for styles, periods, and historic
ornament.

HISTORY OF ORNAMENT, ANCIENT AND MEDIEVAL, A. D. F. Hamlin. 393 pp.
The Century Company
An excellent book for the student of design to consult for period styles
and ornament.

NATURE AND ORNAMENT, Lewis F. Day
Design suggestions in growing plants.

STYLES OF ORNAMENT, Alexander Speltz. Grosset & Dunlap
Profusely illustrated; invaluable to the designer of metal objects.

THE PLANT IN ART AND INDUSTRY, A. Seder
Die Planze in Kunst und Gewerbe. Superb plates showing naturalistic
studies and stylized patterns.

STONES

A BOOK OF PRECIOUS STONES, J. Wodiska
The identification of gem materials and an account of their scientific,
commercial, artistic and historical aspects.

AN ENCYCLOPEDIA OF GEMS, H. E. Briggs
The classification and analysis of gem minerals with a chapter on manufactured and natural gems.

CURIOUS LORE OF PRECIOUS STONES, THE, George F. Kunz
A description of the different ways in which precious stones have been
used down through history, against a background of folklore and
mysticism.

DICTIONARY OF GEMS AND GEMOLOGY, R. M. Shipley
An international reference book for the gemological profession.

GEM CUTTERS CRAFT, L. Claremont
The identification, history and processing of gem stones.

GEMS AND GEM MINERALS, E. H. Kraus
Discusses forms, properties, formation and characteristics of gems, including cutting and polishing.

GEMS AND PRECIOUS STONES, George F. Kunz
Deals with the talismanic and supposedly healing virtues of stones, precious and otherwise.

JEWELRY, GEM CUTTING AND METALCRAFT, W. T. Baxter. McGraw-Hill Book Co.
A textbook for the student and home craftsman.

REVISED LAPIDARY HANDBOOK, J. H. Howard
Practical instruction in all kinds of gem cutting for the beginner.

THE BOOK OF PEARLS, George F. Kunz
One of the most comprehensive books on the subject.

HISTORIC LITERATURE

ANTIQUE JEWELRY AND TRINKETS, F. W. Burgess
A history of the jewelers' art as it developed from the prehistoric age to modern times.

CHATS ON OLD JEWELRY AND TRINKETS, M. Percival
A brief history of jewelry with additional chapters on cameos and intaglios, precious stones and pastes.

FINGER RING LORE, William Jones
It goes beyond superstition, it is a branch of archeology, embracing incidents, historic and social, from the early times with invaluable examples of Glyptic Art; elucidating obscure points in the creeds and general usages of the past, types for artistic imitation, besides supplying links to fix particular times and events.

5000 YEARS OF GEMS AND JEWELRY, Frances Rogers and Alice Beard. Frederick A. Stokes Company
Historical development of the craft from the beginning of time. The best craftsmen of each period in art are presented. The second volume is devoted to the discussion of gems, their substance, history, comparative value, methods of cutting, etc.

GOLDSMITHS' AND SILVERSMITHS' WORK, Nelson Dawson. Methuen & Company; G. P. Putnam's Sons
The beauty of the work of the artisan, accounts of peasant jewelry, the traditions of the historic hollow ware such as the chalice, pyx, and drinking vessels form part of the many interesting items discussed in this book.

HISTORY AND POETRY OF FINGER RINGS, THE, Charles Edwards. Redfield
The history and lore of the finger ring from early times.

NAVAJO SILVER, Arthur Woodward
Of interest to the student doing research on American History, to the student of design, and the craftsman in jewelry.

RINGS FOR THE FINGERS, George F. Kunz
The origin and history of the finger ring.

JEWELRY DICTIONARY. Published by the Jewelers' Circular—Keystone
A comprehensive lexicon of trade and technical terms.

JEWELERS' POCKET REFERENCE BOOK, R. M. Shipley
An up-to-date guidebook for jewelry buyers and salesmen.

Additional Reference Books (1966)

JEWELRY MAKING AND DESIGN, ENAMELING

GOLD GRANULATIONS, John Paul Miller, "Craft Horizon," April, 1957.

HANDWROUGHT JEWELRY, Lois E. Franke and W. L. Udell. New York: McKnight & McKnight Publishers, 1962.

JEWELRY MAKING AND ENAMELING, Harry Zarchy. New York: Alfred A. Knopf, Inc., 1959.

JEWELRY MAKING AS AN ART EXPRESSION, D. Kenneth Winebrenner. Scranton: International Textbook Co., 1953.

JEWELRY MAKING FOR THE BEGINNING CRAFTSMAN, Greta Pack. Princeton: D. Van Nostrand Co., Inc., 1957.

JEWELRY MAKING FOR SCHOOLS, TRADESMEN, AND CRAFTSMEN, Murray Bovin. Forest Hills, New York: Murray Bovin, 1955.

JEWELRY MAKING FOR FUN AND PROFIT, Helen Clegg and Mary Larom. New York: David McKay Co., Inc., 1951.

ART METAL AND JEWELRY, Louise James Haas. White Plains, New York: L. J. Haas, 1940.

HOW TO MAKE MODERN JEWELRY, Charles J. Martin & Victor D'Amico. New York: Museum of Art, Doubleday and Co., Inc., 1949.

SIMPLE JEWELRY, Richard L. B. Rathbone. New York: D. Van Nostrand Co., Inc., 1915.

CABOCHON JEWELRY MAKING, Arthur Sanger. Peoria, Illinois: Chas. A. Bennett Co., Inc., 1951.

DESIGNING AND MAKING HANDWROUGHT JEWELRY, Joseph F. Shoenfelt. New York: McGraw-Hill Book Co., Inc., 1960.

HAND MADE JEWELRY, Louis Wiener. Princeton: D. Van Nostrand Co., Inc., 1960.

THE DESIGN AND CREATION OF JEWELRY, Robert Von Neumann. Philadelphia: Chilton Company Book Division, 1961.

JEWELRY AND SILVER DESIGNS

CONTEMPORARY JEWELLERY AND SILVER DESIGNS.

STONES FOR JEWELRY

THE WORLD OF JEWEL STONES, Michael Weinstein. New York: Sheridan House, Inc., 1958.

JEWELRY REPAIR

THE JEWELRY MANUAL, Richard Allen Hardy. Princeton: D. Van Nostrand Co., Inc., 1941.

HISTORIC LITERATURE

YOUR JEWELRY, Leslie J. Auld. London: Sylvan Press, 1933.

FOUR CENTURIES OF EUROPEAN JEWELLERY, Ernle Dusgate Selby Bradford. London: Country Life, 1953.

ANTIQUE JEWELRY, Ada Darling. Watkins Glen, New York: Century House Americana, 1953.

VICTORIAN JEWELRY, Margaret Cameron Flower. New York: Duell, Sloan and Pearce, Inc., 1951.

JEWELS AND THE WOMAN, Marianne Ostier. New York: Horizon Press, Inc., 1958.

THE ROMANCE OF THE JEWEL, Francis Powys Stopford. London: printed for private circulation, 1920.

JEWELS OF ROMANCE AND RENOWN, Mary Abbott. London: T. W. Laurie, 1933.

MAGICAL JEWELS OF THE MIDDLE AGES AND THE RENAISSANCE, Joan Evans. Oxford, England: Clarendon Press, 1922.

THE BROOCHES OF MANY NATIONS, Harriet A. Heaton. Nottingham, England: Murray's Nottingham Book Co., Ltd., 1904.

INDIAN JEWELLERY, ORNAMENTS AND DECORATIVE DESIGNS, Jamila Brij Bhushan. Bombay: Tataporevala Sons, 1954. Reprinted by Tudor Publishing Co., 1963.

JEWELRY AND GOLD WORK, Charles Densmore Curtis. Rome: American Society for the Excavation of Sardie, Vol. XIII, 1925.

THE GOLDSMITH OF FLORENCE, Katharine Gibson. New York: The Macmillan Co., 1929.

GEMS AND JEWELRY TODAY, Marcus Baerwald. New York: Sheridan House, Inc., 1958.

A TREASURY OF JEWELS AND GEMS, Mona Curran. New York, Emerson Books, Inc., 1962.

THE MAGIC OF JEWELS AND CHARMS, George Frederick Kunz.   Philadelphia: J. B. Lippincott Co., 1915.

JEWELLERY, Cyril Davenport.   Chicago: A. C. McClurg & Co., 1908.

THE LIFE OF BENVENUTO CELLINI, Benvenuto Cellini, translated by John Addington Symonds.   New York: Brentano, 1913.

THE ETRUSCANS AND THEIR JEWELRY, Antonio Cirino.   Rhode Island School of Design Library, 1953.

THE ARNOLD SILVER, Antonio Cirino.   Boston: privately issued, Library of Boston Museum of Fine Arts, John Hay Library of Brown University, 1959.

FILIGREE JEWELRY FROM ANCIENT TIMES, Antonio Cirino.   Providence, Rhode Island: Van Dell Corporation, 1959.

JEWELRY DESIGNING VERSUS TARIFF, Antonio Cirino.   Providence, Rhode Island, "The Manufacturing Jeweler," July 17, 1933.

Index

A CATALOGUE OF SELECTED DOVER BOOKS
IN ALL FIELDS OF INTEREST

A CATALOGUE OF SELECTED DOVER BOOKS
IN ALL FIELDS OF INTEREST

AMERICA'S OLD MASTERS, James T. Flexner. Four men emerged unexpectedly from provincial 18th century America to leadership in European art: Benjamin West, J. S. Copley, C. R. Peale, Gilbert Stuart. Brilliant coverage of lives and contributions. Revised, 1967 edition. 69 plates. 365pp. of text.
21806-6 Paperbound $3.00

FIRST FLOWERS OF OUR WILDERNESS: AMERICAN PAINTING, THE COLONIAL PERIOD, James T. Flexner. Painters, and regional painting traditions from earliest Colonial times up to the emergence of Copley, West and Peale Sr., Foster, Gustavus Hesselius, Feke, John Smibert and many anonymous painters in the primitive manner. Engaging presentation, with 162 illustrations. xxii + 368pp.
22180-6 Paperbound $3.50

THE LIGHT OF DISTANT SKIES: AMERICAN PAINTING, 1760-1835, James T. Flexner. The great generation of early American painters goes to Europe to learn and to teach: West, Copley, Gilbert Stuart and others. Allston, Trumbull, Morse; also contemporary American painters—primitives, derivatives, academics—who remained in America. 102 illustrations. xiii + 306pp. 22179-2 Paperbound $3.50

A HISTORY OF THE RISE AND PROGRESS OF THE ARTS OF DESIGN IN THE UNITED STATES, William Dunlap. Much the richest mine of information on early American painters, sculptors, architects, engravers, miniaturists, etc. The only source of information for scores of artists, the major primary source for many others. Unabridged reprint of rare original 1834 edition, with new introduction by James T. Flexner, and 394 new illustrations. Edited by Rita Weiss. 6⅝ x 9⅝.
21695-0, 21696-9, 21697-7 Three volumes, Paperbound $15 .00

EPOCHS OF CHINESE AND JAPANESE ART, Ernest F. Fenollosa. From primitive Chinese art to the 20th century, thorough history, explanation of every important art period and form, including Japanese woodcuts; main stress on China and Japan, but Tibet, Korea also included. Still unexcelled for its detailed, rich coverage of cultural background, aesthetic elements, diffusion studies, particularly of the historical period. 2nd, 1913 edition. 242 illustrations. lii + 439pp. of text.
20364-6, 20365-4 Two volumes, Paperbound $6.00

THE GENTLE ART OF MAKING ENEMIES, James A. M. Whistler. Greatest wit of his day deflates Oscar Wilde, Ruskin, Swinburne; strikes back at inane critics, exhibitions, art journalism; aesthetics of impressionist revolution in most striking form. Highly readable classic by great painter. Reproduction of edition designed by Whistler. Introduction by Alfred Werner. xxxvi + 334pp.
21875-9 Paperbound $3.00

ALPHABETS AND ORNAMENTS, Ernst Lehner. Well-known pictorial source for decorative alphabets, script examples, cartouches, frames, decorative title pages, calligraphic initials, borders, similar material. 14th to 19th century, mostly European. Useful in almost any graphic arts designing, varied styles. 750 illustrations. 256pp. 7 x 10.   21905-4 Paperbound $4.00

PAINTING: A CREATIVE APPROACH, Norman Colquhoun. For the beginner simple guide provides an instructive approach to painting: major stumbling blocks for beginner; overcoming them, technical points; paints and pigments; oil painting; watercolor and other media and color. New section on "plastic" paints. Glossary. Formerly *Paint Your Own Pictures*. 221pp.   22000-1 Paperbound $1.75

THE ENJOYMENT AND USE OF COLOR, Walter Sargent. Explanation of the relations between colors themselves and between colors in nature and art, including hundreds of little-known facts about color values, intensities, effects of high and low illumination, complementary colors. Many practical hints for painters, references to great masters. 7 color plates, 29 illustrations. x + 274pp.
20944-X Paperbound $3.00

THE NOTEBOOKS OF LEONARDO DA VINCI, compiled and edited by Jean Paul Richter. 1566 extracts from original manuscripts reveal the full range of Leonardo's versatile genius: all his writings on painting, sculpture, architecture, anatomy, astronomy, geography, topography, physiology, mining, music, etc., in both Italian and English, with 186 plates of manuscript pages and more than 500 additional drawings. Includes studies for the Last Supper, the lost Sforza monument, and other works. Total of xlvii + 866pp. 7⅞ x 10¾.
22572-0, 22573-9 Two volumes, Paperbound $12.00

MONTGOMERY WARD CATALOGUE OF 1895. Tea gowns, yards of flannel and pillow-case lace, stereoscopes, books of gospel hymns, the New Improved Singer Sewing Machine, side saddles, milk skimmers, straight-edged razors, high-button shoes, spittoons, and on and on . . . listing some 25,000 items, practically all illustrated. Essential to the shoppers of the 1890's, it is our truest record of the spirit of the period. Unaltered reprint of Issue No. 57, Spring and Summer 1895. Introduction by Boris Emmet. Innumerable illustrations. xiii + 624pp. 8½ x 11⅝.
22377-9 Paperbound $8.50

THE CRYSTAL PALACE EXHIBITION ILLUSTRATED CATALOGUE (LONDON, 1851). One of the wonders of the modern world—the Crystal Palace Exhibition in which all the nations of the civilized world exhibited their achievements in the arts and sciences—presented in an equally important illustrated catalogue. More than 1700 items pictured with accompanying text—ceramics, textiles, cast-iron work, carpets, pianos, sleds, razors, wall-papers, billiard tables, beehives, silverware and hundreds of other artifacts—represent the focal point of Victorian culture in the Western World. Probably the largest collection of Victorian decorative art ever assembled— indispensable for antiquarians and designers. Unabridged republication of the Art-Journal Catalogue of the Great Exhibition of 1851, with all terminal essays. New introduction by John Gloag, F.S.A. xxxiv + 426pp. 9 x 12.
22503-8 Paperbound $5.00

AGAINST THE GRAIN (A REBOURS), Joris K. Huysmans. Filled with weird images, evidences of a bizarre imagination, exotic experiments with hallucinatory drugs, rich tastes and smells and the diversions of its sybarite hero Duc Jean des Esseintes, this classic novel pushed 19th-century literary decadence to its limits. Full unabridged edition. Do not confuse this with abridged editions generally sold. Introduction by Havelock Ellis. xlix + 206pp. 22190-3 Paperbound $2.50

VARIORUM SHAKESPEARE: HAMLET. Edited by Horace H. Furness; a landmark of American scholarship. Exhaustive footnotes and appendices treat all doubtful words and phrases, as well as suggested critical emendations throughout the play's history. First volume contains editor's own text, collated with all Quartos and Folios. Second volume contains full first Quarto, translations of Shakespeare's sources (Belleforest, and Saxo Grammaticus), Der Bestrafte Brudermord, and many essays on critical and historical points of interest by major authorities of past and present. Includes details of staging and costuming over the years. By far the best edition available for serious students of Shakespeare. Total of xx + 905pp. 21004-9, 21005-7, 2 volumes, Paperbound $7.00

A LIFE OF WILLIAM SHAKESPEARE, Sir Sidney Lee. This is the standard life of Shakespeare, summarizing everything known about Shakespeare and his plays. Incredibly rich in material, broad in coverage, clear and judicious, it has served thousands as the best introduction to Shakespeare. 1931 edition. 9 plates. xxix + 792pp. 21967-4 Paperbound $4.50

MASTERS OF THE DRAMA, John Gassner. Most comprehensive history of the drama in print, covering every tradition from Greeks to modern Europe and America, including India, Far East, etc. Covers more than 800 dramatists, 2000 plays, with biographical material, plot summaries, theatre history, criticism, etc. "Best of its kind in English," *New Republic*. 77 illustrations. xxii + 890pp. 20100-7 Clothbound $10.00

THE EVOLUTION OF THE ENGLISH LANGUAGE, George McKnight. The growth of English, from the 14th century to the present. Unusual, non-technical account presents basic information in very interesting form: sound shifts, change in grammar and syntax, vocabulary growth, similar topics. Abundantly illustrated with quotations. Formerly *Modern English in the Making*. xii + 590pp. 21932-1 Paperbound $3.50

AN ETYMOLOGICAL DICTIONARY OF MODERN ENGLISH, Ernest Weekley. Fullest, richest work of its sort, by foremost British lexicographer. Detailed word histories, including many colloquial and archaic words; extensive quotations. Do not confuse this with the Concise Etymological Dictionary, which is much abridged. Total of xxvii + 830pp. 6½ x 9¼. 21873-2, 21874-0 Two volumes, Paperbound $7.90

FLATLAND: A ROMANCE OF MANY DIMENSIONS, E. A. Abbott. Classic of science-fiction explores ramifications of life in a two-dimensional world, and what happens when a three-dimensional being intrudes. Amusing reading, but also useful as introduction to thought about hyperspace. Introduction by Banesh Hoffmann. 16 illustrations. xx + 103pp. 20001-9 Paperbound $1.00

THE RED FAIRY BOOK, Andrew Lang. Lang's color fairy books have long been children's favorites. This volume includes Rapunzel, Jack and the Bean-stalk and 35 other stories, familiar and unfamiliar. 4 plates, 93 illustrations x + 367pp.
21673-X Paperbound $2.50

THE BLUE FAIRY BOOK, Andrew Lang. Lang's tales come from all countries and all times. Here are 37 tales from Grimm, the Arabian Nights, Greek Mythology, and other fascinating sources. 8 plates, 130 illustrations. xi + 390pp.
21437-0 Paperbound $2.75

HOUSEHOLD STORIES BY THE BROTHERS GRIMM. Classic English-language edition of the well-known tales — Rumpelstiltskin, Snow White, Hansel and Gretel, The Twelve Brothers, Faithful John, Rapunzel, Tom Thumb (52 stories in all). Translated into simple, straightforward English by Lucy Crane. Ornamented with headpieces, vignettes, elaborate decorative initials and a dozen full-page illustrations by Walter Crane. x + 269pp.
21080-4 Paperbound **$2.00**

THE MERRY ADVENTURES OF ROBIN HOOD, Howard Pyle. The finest modern versions of the traditional ballads and tales about the great English outlaw. Howard Pyle's complete prose version, with every word, every illustration of the first edition. Do not confuse this facsimile of the original (1883) with modern editions that change text or illustrations. 23 plates plus many page decorations. xxii + 296pp.
22043-5 Paperbound $2.75

THE STORY OF KING ARTHUR AND HIS KNIGHTS, Howard Pyle. The finest children's version of the life of King Arthur; brilliantly retold by Pyle, with 48 of his most imaginative illustrations. xviii + 313pp. 6⅛ x 9¼.
21445-1 Paperbound $2.50

THE WONDERFUL WIZARD OF OZ, L. Frank Baum. America's finest children's book in facsimile of first edition with all Denslow illustrations in full color. The edition a child should have. Introduction by Martin Gardner. 23 color plates, scores of drawings. iv + 267pp.
20691-2 Paperbound **$3.50**

THE MARVELOUS LAND OF OZ, L. Frank Baum. The second Oz book, every bit as imaginative as the Wizard. The hero is a boy named Tip, but the Scarecrow and the Tin Woodman are back, as is the Oz magic. 16 color plates, 120 drawings by John R. Neill. 287pp.
20692-0 Paperbound $2.50

THE MAGICAL MONARCH OF MO, L. Frank Baum. Remarkable adventures in a land even stranger than Oz. The best of Baum's books not in the Oz series. 15 color plates and dozens of drawings by Frank Verbeck. xviii + 237pp.
21892-9 Paperbound $2.25

THE BAD CHILD'S BOOK OF BEASTS, MORE BEASTS FOR WORSE CHILDREN, A MORAL ALPHABET, Hilaire Belloc. Three complete humor classics in one volume. Be kind to the frog, and do not call him names . . . and 28 other whimsical animals. Familiar favorites and some not so well known. Illustrated by Basil Blackwell. 156pp.
(USO) 20749-8 Paperbound $1.50

"ESSENTIAL GRAMMAR" SERIES

All you really need to know about modern, colloquial grammar. Many educational shortcuts help you learn faster, understand better. Detailed cognate lists teach you to recognize similarities between English and foreign words and roots—make learning vocabulary easy and interesting. Excellent for independent study or as a supplement to record courses.

ESSENTIAL FRENCH GRAMMAR, Seymour Resnick. 2500-item cognate list. 159pp.
(EBE) 20419-7 Paperbound $1.50

ESSENTIAL GERMAN GRAMMAR, Guy Stern and Everett F. Bleiler. Unusual shortcuts on noun declension, word order, compound verbs. 124pp.
(EBE) 20422-7 Paperbound $1.25

ESSENTIAL ITALIAN GRAMMAR, Olga Ragusa. 111pp.
(EBE) 20779-X Paperbound $1.25

ESSENTIAL JAPANESE GRAMMAR, Everett F. Bleiler. In Romaji transcription; no characters needed. Japanese grammar is regular and simple. 156pp.
21027-8 Paperbound $1.50

ESSENTIAL PORTUGUESE GRAMMAR, Alexander da R. Prista. vi + 114pp.
21650-0 Paperbound $1.35

ESSENTIAL SPANISH GRAMMAR, Seymour Resnick. 2500 word cognate list. 115pp.
(EBE) 20780-3 Paperbound $1.25

ESSENTIAL ENGLISH GRAMMAR, Philip Gucker. Combines best features of modern, functional and traditional approaches. For refresher, class use, home study. x + 177pp.
21649-7 Paperbound $1.75

A PHRASE AND SENTENCE DICTIONARY OF SPOKEN SPANISH. Prepared for U. S. War Department by U. S. linguists. As above, unit is idiom, phrase or sentence rather than word. English-Spanish and Spanish-English sections contain modern equivalents of over 18,000 sentences. Introduction and appendix as above. iv + 513pp.
20495-2 Paperbound $3.50

A PHRASE AND SENTENCE DICTIONARY OF SPOKEN RUSSIAN. Dictionary prepared for U. S. War Department by U. S. linguists. Basic unit is not the word, but the idiom, phrase or sentence. English-Russian and Russian-English sections contain modern equivalents for over 30,000 phrases. Grammatical introduction covers phonetics, writing, syntax. Appendix of word lists for food, numbers, geographical names, etc. vi + 573 pp. 6⅛ x 9¼. 20496-0 Paperbound $5.50

CONVERSATIONAL CHINESE FOR BEGINNERS, Morris Swadesh. Phonetic system, beginner's course in Pai Hua Mandarin Chinese covering most important, most useful speech patterns. Emphasis on modern colloquial usage. Formerly *Chinese in Your Pocket*. xvi + 158pp.
21123-1 Paperbound $1.75

INCIDENTS OF TRAVEL IN YUCATAN, John L. Stephens. Classic (1843) exploration of jungles of Yucatan, looking for evidences of Maya civilization. Stephens found many ruins; comments on travel adventures, Mexican and Indian culture. 127 striking illustrations by F. Catherwood. Total of 669 pp.
20926-1, 20927-X Two volumes, Paperbound $5.50

INCIDENTS OF TRAVEL IN CENTRAL AMERICA, CHIAPAS, AND YUCATAN, John L. Stephens. An exciting travel journal and an important classic of archeology. Narrative relates his almost single-handed discovery of the Mayan culture, and exploration of the ruined cities of Copan, Palenque, Utatlan and others; the monuments they dug from the earth, the temples buried in the jungle, the customs of poverty-stricken Indians living a stone's throw from the ruined palaces. 115 drawings by F. Catherwood. Portrait of Stephens. xii + 812pp.
22404-X, 22405-8 Two volumes, Paperbound $6.00

A NEW VOYAGE ROUND THE WORLD, William Dampier. Late 17-century naturalist joined the pirates of the Spanish Main to gather information; remarkably vivid account of buccaneers, pirates; detailed, accurate account of botany, zoology, ethnography of lands visited. Probably the most important early English voyage, enormous implications for British exploration, trade, colonial policy. Also most interesting reading. Argonaut edition, introduction by Sir Albert Gray. New introduction by Percy Adams. 6 plates, 7 illustrations. xlvii + 376pp. 6½ x 9¼.
21900-3 Paperbound $3.00

INTERNATIONAL AIRLINE PHRASE BOOK IN SIX LANGUAGES, Joseph W. Bátor. Important phrases and sentences in English paralleled with French, German, Portuguese, Italian, Spanish equivalents, covering all possible airport-travel situations; created for airline personnel as well as tourist by Language Chief, Pan American Airlines. xiv + 204pp.
22017-6 Paperbound $2.25

STAGE COACH AND TAVERN DAYS, Alice Morse Earle. Detailed, lively account of the early days of taverns; their uses and importance in the social, political and military life; furnishings and decorations; locations; food and drink; tavern signs, etc. Second half covers every aspect of early travel; the roads, coaches, drivers, etc. Nostalgic, charming, packed with fascinating material. 157 illustrations, mostly photographs. xiv + 449pp.
22518-6 Paperbound $4.00

NORSE DISCOVERIES AND EXPLORATIONS IN NORTH AMERICA, Hjalmar R. Holand. The perplexing Kensington Stone, found in Minnesota at the end of the 19th century. Is it a record of a Scandinavian expedition to North America in the 14th century? Or is it one of the most successful hoaxes in history. A scientific detective investigation. Formerly *Westward from Vinland*. 31 photographs, 17 figures. x + 354pp.
22014-1 Paperbound $2.75

A BOOK OF OLD MAPS, compiled and edited by Emerson D. Fite and Archibald Freeman. 74 old maps offer an unusual survey of the discovery, settlement and growth of America down to the close of the Revolutionary war: maps showing Norse settlements in Greenland, the explorations of Columbus, Verrazano, Cabot, Champlain, Joliet, Drake, Hudson, etc., campaigns of Revolutionary war battles, and much more. Each map is accompanied by a brief historical essay. xvi + 299pp. 11 x 13¾.
22084-2 Paperbound $7.00

THE PRINCIPLES OF PSYCHOLOGY, William James. The famous long course, complete and unabridged. Stream of thought, time perception, memory, experimental methods—these are only some of the concerns of a work that was years ahead of its time and still valid, interesting, useful. 94 figures. Total of xviii + 1391pp.
20381-6, 20382-4 Two volumes, Paperbound $9.00

THE STRANGE STORY OF THE QUANTUM, Banesh Hoffmann. Non-mathematical but thorough explanation of work of Planck, Einstein, Bohr, Pauli, de Broglie, Schrödinger, Heisenberg, Dirac, Feynman, etc. No technical background needed. "Of books attempting such an account, this is the best," Henry Margenau, Yale. 40-page "Postscript 1959." xii + 285pp. 20518-5 Paperbound $3.00

THE RISE OF THE NEW PHYSICS, A. d'Abro. Most thorough explanation in print of central core of mathematical physics, both classical and modern; from Newton to Dirac and Heisenberg. Both history and exposition; philosophy of science, causality, explanations of higher mathematics, analytical mechanics, electromagnetism, thermodynamics, phase rule, special and general relativity, matrices. No higher mathematics needed to follow exposition, though treatment is elementary to intermediate in level. Recommended to serious student who wishes verbal understanding. 97 illustrations. xvii + 982pp. 20003-5, 20004-3 Two volumes, Paperbound $10.00

GREAT IDEAS OF OPERATIONS RESEARCH, Jagjit Singh. Easily followed non-technical explanation of mathematical tools, aims, results: statistics, linear programming, game theory, queueing theory, Monte Carlo simulation, etc. Uses only elementary mathematics. Many case studies, several analyzed in detail. Clarity, breadth make this excellent for specialist in another field who wishes background. 41 figures. x + 228pp. 21886-4 Paperbound $2.50

GREAT IDEAS OF MODERN MATHEMATICS: THEIR NATURE AND USE, Jagjit Singh. Internationally famous expositor, winner of Unesco's Kalinga Award for science popularization explains verbally such topics as differential equations, matrices, groups, sets, transformations, mathematical logic and other important modern mathematics, as well as use in physics, astrophysics, and similar fields. Superb exposition for layman, scientist in other areas. viii + 312pp.
20587-8 Paperbound $2.75

GREAT IDEAS IN INFORMATION THEORY, LANGUAGE AND CYBERNETICS, Jagjit Singh. The analog and digital computers, how they work, how they are like and unlike the human brain, the men who developed them, their future applications, computer terminology. An essential book for today, even for readers with little math. Some mathematical demonstrations included for more advanced readers. 118 figures. Tables. ix + 338pp. 21694-2 Paperbound $2.50

CHANCE, LUCK AND STATISTICS, Horace C. Levinson. Non-mathematical presentation of fundamentals of probability theory and science of statistics and their applications. Games of chance, betting odds, misuse of statistics, normal and skew distributions, birth rates, stock speculation, insurance. Enlarged edition. Formerly "The Science of Chance." xiii + 357pp. 21007-3 Paperbound $2.50

MATHEMATICAL PUZZLES FOR BEGINNERS AND ENTHUSIASTS, Geoffrey Mott-Smith. 189 puzzles from easy to difficult—involving arithmetic, logic, algebra, properties of digits, probability, etc.—for enjoyment and mental stimulus. Explanation of mathematical principles behind the puzzles. 135 illustrations. viii + 248pp.
20198-8 Paperbound $2.00

PAPER FOLDING FOR BEGINNERS, William D. Murray and Francis J. Rigney. Easiest book on the market, clearest instructions on making interesting, beautiful origami. Sail boats, cups, roosters, frogs that move legs, bonbon boxes, standing birds, etc. 40 projects; more than 275 diagrams and photographs. 94pp.
20713-7 Paperbound $1.00

TRICKS AND GAMES ON THE POOL TABLE, Fred Herrmann. 79 tricks and games—some solitaires, some for two or more players, some competitive games—to entertain you between formal games. Mystifying shots and throws, unusual caroms, tricks involving such props as cork, coins, a hat, etc. Formerly *Fun on the Pool Table.* 77 figures. 95pp.
21814-7 Paperbound $1.25

HAND SHADOWS TO BE THROWN UPON THE WALL: A SERIES OF NOVEL AND AMUSING FIGURES FORMED BY THE HAND, Henry Bursill. Delightful picturebook from great-grandfather's day shows how to make 18 different hand shadows: a bird that flies, duck that quacks, dog that wags his tail, camel, goose, deer, boy, turtle, etc. Only book of its sort. vi + 33pp. 6½ x 9¼. 21779-5 Paperbound $1.00

WHITTLING AND WOODCARVING, E. J. Tangerman. 18th printing of best book on market. "If you can cut a potato you can carve" toys and puzzles, chains, chessmen, caricatures, masks, frames, woodcut blocks, surface patterns, much more. Information on tools, woods, techniques. Also goes into serious wood sculpture from Middle Ages to present, East and West. 464 photos, figures. x + 293pp.
20965-2 Paperbound $2.50

HISTORY OF PHILOSOPHY, Julián Marías. Possibly the clearest, most easily followed, best planned, most useful one-volume history of philosophy on the market; neither skimpy nor overfull. Full details on system of every major philosopher and dozens of less important thinkers from pre-Socratics up to Existentialism and later. Strong on many European figures usually omitted. Has gone through dozens of editions in Europe. 1966 edition, translated by Stanley Appelbaum and Clarence Strowbridge. xviii + 505pp. 21739-6 Paperbound $3.50

YOGA: A SCIENTIFIC EVALUATION, Kovoor T. Behanan. Scientific but non-technical study of physiological results of yoga exercises; done under auspices of Yale U. Relations to Indian thought, to psychoanalysis, etc. 16 photos. xxiii + 270pp.
20505-3 Paperbound $2.50

Prices subject to change without notice.

Available at your book dealer or write for free catalogue to Dept. GI, Dover Publications, Inc., 180 Varick St., N. Y., N. Y. 10014. Dover publishes more than 150 books each year on science, elementary and advanced mathematics, biology, music, art, literary history, social sciences and other areas.